D0563929

The Wolf in CIO's Clothing

A Machiavellian Strategy for Successful IT Leadership

TINA NUNNO

Gartner, Inc.

Additional Books by Gartner Authors

Learn more at gartner.com/books

Gamify: How Gamification Motivates People to Do Extraordinary Things
Brian Burke
Bibliomotion, Inc., 2014

The Digital Edge:
Exploiting Information and Technology for Business Advantage
Mark P. McDonald and Andy Rowsell-Jones
Gartner, Inc., 2012, eBook

The Social Organization:
How to Use Social Media to Tap the Collective Genius of Your Customers and Employees
Anthony J. Bradley and Mark P. McDonald
Harvard Business Review Press, 2011

The CIO Edge:
Seven Leadership Skills You Need to Drive Results
Graham Waller (Gartner), George Hallenbeck
(Korn/Ferry) and Karen Rubenstrunk (Korn/Ferry)
Harvard Business Review Press, 2010

The Real Business of IT:
How CIOs Create and Communicate Value
Richard Hunter (Gartner) and George Westerman,
(MIT)
Harvard Business Press, 2009

Mastering the Hype Cycle: How to Choose the Right Innovation at the Right Time
Jackie Fenn and Mark Raskino
Harvard Business Press, 2008

Are you a Wolf CIO?

As you read this book, consider your own approach to the three Machiavellian disciplines: Power, Manipulation and Warfare. Are you more comfortable on the light or dark side?

Take the Wolf CIO quiz and find out.
www.gartner.com/wolfcio.

First Bibliomotion edition
(previously published by Gartner, Inc.)

Bibliomotion, Inc.
39 Harvard Street
Brookline, MA 02445
Tel: 617-934-2427
www.bibliomotion.com

Copyright © 2015 by Gartner, Inc.

All rights reserved. No part of this publication may be
reproduced in any manner whatsoever without written
permission from the publisher, except in the case of brief
quotations embodied in critical articles or reviews.

Printed in the United States of America

Library of Congress Cataloging-in-Publication Data

Nunno, Tina.
   The wolf in CIO's clothing : a Machiavellian strategy for successful IT leadership /
Tina Nunno. — First Edition.
        pages cm
   Summary: "In The Wolf in CIO's Clothing, Gartner analyst and author Tina Nunno
expands on Machiavelli's metaphor, examining seven animal types and the leadership
attributes of each"— Provided by publisher.
   ISBN 978-1-62956-087-8 (hardback) — ISBN 978-1-62956-088-5 (ebook)
   1. Information technology—Management.   2. Leadership.   I. Title.
HD30.2.N86 2015
004.068'4—dc23
                              2014047443

Dedication

This book is dedicated to my husband Frank. Throughout my travels many people have wondered aloud about what kind of a man would be married to a woman like me. Fortunately for me, the answer is an amazing man who has a great sense of humor, which he needs to deal with me, and who is always supportive of my endeavors, no matter how absurd they are. Without you, this book would not have been possible.

Contents

Introduction

As a leader, do you think of yourself as predator or prey? Are you a wolf or a lamb? In other words, which animal best describes your leadership style? Are you a fighter, a protector, or a formidable ally? Most importantly, what do you stand for and believe in as a person and as a leader? Are you willing to fight for what you believe in, and can you protect the things you value?

These may seem like unusual questions to ask the CIOs, future CIOs, and IT leaders for whom I wrote this book. Your CEOs, CFOs, and colleagues likely don't ask such things of you and probably don't think of you in this way. They are more likely to think of you as a service provider. And they often expect service providers to do what they are told, when they are told to do it, no matter how unreasonable or absurd the request may be.

At the same time, many CEOs and boards of directors recognize the transformational role of technology. They have seen its power to radically change business models and provide extraordinary competitive advantage. They want to use technology creatively and strategically to achieve that competitive advantage and claim to want IT leaders who will break out of the service mold, lead much more aggressively, and work with them to shape a new digital future.

So why isn't it happening? Let's look at the data. In the year since this book was released, more than 4,500 IT executives have taken the Wolf Quiz to learn their Extreme Animal Profile. You can take it at www.gartner.com/wolfquiz, and I encourage you to do so before you read this book. In a recent discussion with a client, I told him that approximately 47 percent of the survey participants exhibited some Wolf-like tendencies. He asked, "So why haven't we made more progress?"

Here is why. CIOs with Wolf leadership tendencies are often told those tendencies are wrong and that they should get back into the service provider box. Unfortunately, many of them comply. Their senior executives and business colleagues, who claim to want IT leaders, miss the service providers who did what they were told. Or, they feel threatened by the new predator on the block rather than welcoming her into the pack.

Neither CIOs nor CEOs understand the real leadership dynamics, which need to change in order for CIOs to succeed and for their enterprises to use technology to win. In order for both of these positive results to occur, CIOs and their colleagues must recognize a few simple realities.

First, predators only partner with other predators. Predators don't partner with prey. Service providers are prey. Predators eat prey. They play with prey. They do not partner with them.

I have spoken with some non-IT executives who have stated, "My CIO is not a leader; he just does what he is told." These executives are pointing out the uncomfortable reality that when we do what others tell us to do, we are rendered invisible. Leaders are not invisible or endlessly malleable, they have a presence all their own.

Second, IT leaders are reluctant to embrace the predator role. Predators are scary; therefore, they must be bad, right? Wrong. Just because you are scary does not mean you are the bad guy. But in tough times, if you are scary, I want you on my side.

I spoke with a female CIO recently who told me, "I am not a Wolf!" She then proceeded to tell me how she recently had dealt with a business colleague who had sent a disparaging e-mail about one of her staff. She marched to his office and explained in no uncertain terms why he would never speak to one of her team members in that manner again. Only after he apologized and promised to behave more appropriately, did she address his IT issue.

I looked at her and said, "You are so Wolfy you have no idea!" She was fiercely protective of her team, and had both the power and ability to draw the line so that she could actually protect them. Very "Wolfy" indeed.

It is important to note that the reverse corollary about scariness is also untrue. Just because you are nice does not mean that you are the good guy or gal.

Consider another recent conversation I had with a *nice* IT executive (you could call him a Dolphin, which we'll get into in a few chapters) who loves his fast-growing company. His challenge was that the workload was so massive, the IT staff turned over on average every twelve to eighteen months. Their untenable workload was due to their inability to say "no." They never refused an IT request. Ever. Why? "We don't want to seem uncooperative or make them unhappy," he told me. I asked what he was doing about it and his response was, "I'm hiring more IT people." This is not the right answer.

Globally, I speak with CIOs on a daily basis who are in this situation. They are nice, well-meaning people who are trying to make others happy. We must recognize that "happy" is not a business goal. Service providers pursue "happy." Leaders pursue growth, competitive advantage, mission enhancement, and cost management.

Unfortunately, nice IT service providers often sacrifice their IT teams and make them unhappy rather than risk making others unhappy. They choose not to, or lack the power to, draw the line to protect their teams, and end up inadvertently putting both their teams and the enterprise at risk. Often, they drown in low-value, reactive work they can't say no to, rather than proactively pursuing strategic initiatives of their own making.

What is the alternative? To be nice *and* scary. Like a Wolf. I encourage you to bring your inner Wolf out to play, to lead, and to protect your team and your enterprise. Let me be clear, this book is not a license to behave recklessly, selfishly, or malevolently. In fact, I purposefully leverage Machiavelli's teachings for your greater good and the good of your enterprise. I'll explain.

I am first-generation Italian. My parents immigrated to the United States when they were adults, and I was born into a large Italian-American community in Connecticut. My people think of conflict as a recreational sport. If my people had created the Olympics, yelling at the dinner table would have been an event. So would protecting the family. We might nearly kill one another on a daily basis, but no outsider messes with the family without serious repercussions.

Most people hear the name Machiavelli and think, "He was bad." My people hear Machiavelli and think, "It is what it is." Niccolo Machiavelli is often misquoted, misunderstood, and misinterpreted. He was a student of history and human behavior. He lived through warfare and experienced the chaos and destruction it created. He witnessed how, when nice people have no skills or power, everything they value falls to people who want what they have. Machiavelli believed in benevolent leaders being willing to fight to create something of value, then fighting to protect it.

Only you can decide what you are willing to fight for, and how to best protect your team and enterprise. The goal of my book is to give you practical tools and a fresh mind-set to help you defend yourself, your team, and your enterprise, and to create something of great value.

Be forewarned. To do so, you may have to go to the dark side. But in doing so, you'll help create a lot more light.

1: Aspire to Be the Machiavellian Wolf CIO

A prince then should know how to employ the nature of man, and that of the beasts as well... It being necessary for a prince to know well how to employ the nature of the beasts,

he should be able to assume both that of the fox and that of the lion; for whilst the latter cannot escape the traps laid for him, the former cannot defend himself against the wolves.

A prince should be a fox, to know the traps and snares; and a lion, to be able to frighten the wolves; for those who simply hold to the nature of the lion do not understand their business.

Machiavelli, *The Prince*

Extreme situations require animal inspiration

Machiavelli advised that a leader should think like an animal because leaders are often embattled. Traditional management research advises that if CIOs follow appropriate processes, procedures and methodology, they should not encounter serious problems. Unfortunately, this simply is not true. Reality demonstrates that CIOs are often challenged by the extraordinary rate of change in IT, increased expectations, and ever-growing demand in the face of shrinking revenue and resources. Often, the more extreme the expectations are of IT in the enterprise, the more extreme the potential conflicts for the CIO.

Today's CIO should aspire to be a Wolf. Machiavelli advised that leaders should take inspiration from two "beasts": the fox to avoid the traps and the lion to scare away the wolves. But for CIOs the ultimate animal is the Wolf — an ideal balance of an intelligent, social creature that can inspire loyal followership and create group affinity; and the ruthless predator that can lead a pack of strong fighters, win in a competitive environment and command a large territory.

CIOs must display all of these qualities to lead highly complex IT organizations with an evolving purview as IT capabilities expand reach and range globally through information, mobility and social media. The territory of the CIO is no longer the basement data center; it now has the potential to reach as far as the technology does. Yet as with the Roman Empire, with a greater territory to protect and maintain comes greater risks.

Consider the following scenario. A CIO's colleagues complain: "We don't get enough IT, or any IT quickly enough, or cheaply enough, and why don't we have some clouds, or really big data or a digital strategy, and why isn't IT driving competitive advantage? I have a friend who told me he has a CIO who does all of this for a fraction of the money that we are spending, and it's all available on their tablets and smartphones. Why can't the CIO simply do what we ask of IT when we ask it, or preferably, before we think of it?"

Sound familiar? When confronted with stakeholders who are unhappy with or critical of IT performance, CIOs have traditionally relied upon reasonable arguments such as: *IT is underfunded, understaffed, not included in strategic meetings or nonstrategic meetings for that matter, and how can we possibly deliver something you didn't ask for and did not know that you wanted until today? And no, it's not possible for me to deliver stunning innovation and emerging technologies to you when I'm busy putting out fires on my underfunded legacy systems while you are allowing other parts of the organization to spend money like water on IT, then throw it over the wall for us to maintain, and we can't keep up. What? You want a new CIO? Didn't you hear what I just said? Wait; let me explain it again...*

Don't bring data to a knife fight

The data-driven, empirical nature of CIOs is a tremendous strength. It helps them deal with the complex and detailed nature of IT, which is often difficult for colleagues in other business areas to comprehend. It can be a strength when dealing with other colleagues who believe in data-driven, empirical decision making. Unfortunately, while many of us are fortunate that our stakeholders are data-driven some of the time, few CIOs can say that their stakeholders are data-driven all of the time. Often, organizational politics accelerate and "rational" decision making is sacrificed in favor of basic survival instincts when enterprises are under stress from declining revenue, decreasing budgets or increased competition. In these situations, data often simply doesn't work.

To be ready for any eventuality, a CIO must be a Wolf. Wolves are predators. Nothing in the animal kingdom eats a Wolf for food. Unfortunately, if you bring data to a knife fight, you are acting like prey and will risk ending up as food.

What animal would you choose to describe yourself?

The animal you choose might be a nice fluffy bunny rabbit. Rabbits are lovely creatures, and very likable. Unfortunately, they are prey and almost every species in the animal kingdom can eat them. The approach many CIOs have taken to combat hostile stakeholders can best be described as, "CIOs are friends, not food." This approach is admirable. These CIOs aspire to be likable and will argue that they are just here to enable the business and support them in any way that they can. They think if everyone would just play together nicely in the pond, then all kinds of strategic value from IT would soon appear.

This approach often works — until it doesn't. When something goes wrong, usually an IT-related disappointment, the environment around the CIO and IT can become hostile. Sometimes this is justified, and sometimes not. In other cases, IT may overreach its traditional territory in the enterprise by doing something extremely successful that threatens the territory of a colleague. This has become true of marketing, sales and customer management, where digital technologies have blurred the traditional lines between IT and other business units. Reactions from colleagues can be hostile rather than appreciative, and a CIO must have a wide array of tools with which to respond.

Wolf CIOs are both grey and binary

CIOs with Wolf qualities exhibit a specific set of leadership behaviors and tactics that all CIOs can develop by adjusting their mindsets about conflict and taking calculated risks. Some of these behaviors and tactics look binary and are best described as "the dark side" of leadership and "the light side." Like most wolves in the wild, CIOs with these qualities are a mix of light and dark, and actually appear grey. They can go to binary extremes when they need to, but on the whole, they live in the complex middle, where identifying the "right" thing to do is easier said than done.

Consider Chris, a CIO who came to believe that his direct report Tim was attempting to steal his job. Chris discovered that Tim had been speaking badly about him to his colleagues across the business, and to the CFO to whom Chris reported. Tim had apparently repeatedly stated that he believed he could do a better job than Chris, who he judged to have a number of weaknesses. Chris fired Tim. Did Chris do the right thing? Machiavelli might say yes.

One of the most famous quotes often attributed to Machiavelli was something he never specifically said, "The end justifies the means." But Machiavelli made similar comments and would likely have agreed with the sentiment if "the end" was the good of the republic, rather than personal gain. Machiavelli lived through the horrors of war and chaos, and believed in the role of great leaders to prevent or minimize such tragedies. So Machiavelli might argue that if Chris believed he was acting in the best interest of the business by staying in leadership and firing Tim, then he did what needed to be done. Right versus wrong cannot be empirically determined here; this is a messy grey area.

Wolf CIOs are driven by doing what is best for the enterprise and are willing to make the difficult trade-offs to protect and advance the whole. Leadership is both a privilege and a burden. Chris, like many CIOs who have had to fire others, will have to bear the personal and leadership burden of firing Tim. This is part and parcel of having the privilege of leading the IT department and the people in it. CIOs who are unwilling to accept the burden of difficult tasks may inadvertently place their enterprises, their departments and themselves at risk.

The light side of the Wolf inspires loyalty

Light-side leadership behaviors are positive and inspirational. They create loyal and enthusiastic followership. CIOs need many stakeholders at multiple levels and across multiple business units to cooperate so that they can successfully complete complex IT-related initiatives. Many of the most strategic and high-value initiatives require creativity and enthusiasm both for the initiative and the leader. These include innovations, top-line growth programs and creating new sources of competitive differentiation. When IT initiatives require creativity and inspiration, CIOs should go to the light side.

CIOs must demonstrate that they have the following light-side behaviors:

- Use positive incentives, social skills and collaboration to create loyalty and followership

- Demonstrate a strong sense of values and communicate them clearly to followers

- Listen and show empathy and caring toward others, across all levels of the organization

- Take the high road by knowing when not to engage in battle and live to fight another day
- Display selflessness and strive to give more than to receive
- Aspire to be viewed as inspirational and worthy of being followed

When CIOs engage in such behaviors, followers often feel admiration for the CIO. They feel good about being part of the leader's community and will be loyal and enthusiastic in their work. They respect the CIO's value system, the way they treat others and the goals that they are in pursuit of together. This lighter side of the Wolf creates a real and perceived sense of intimacy between the CIO and the team, behavior that often draws in even more people over time.

Unfortunately, it is not ideal to rely solely upon light-side behaviors. Some staff may not share the CIO's values, and therefore will be uninspired by them. They may have agendas that are more self-focused rather than enterprise-focused, or they may be loyal to another executive and thus find themselves inadvertently in conflict with the CIO's goals. Most importantly, the intimate relationships established in such teams can leave a CIO vulnerable and open to attacks, with few options for defense. As a result, leaders must also build their toolkit of dark-side behaviors.

The dark side of the Wolf inspires fear

Dark-side behaviors are negative and inspire fear. They can bring stray followers in line and prevent assaults on a CIO's territory or team by ensuring that no potential enemy considers them an easy target. Take the example of Chris firing Tim. For good or bad, Chris's actions send a necessary message to other potential usurpers that they should think twice before attempting to usurp the CIO as Tim did. It also sends a message to other executives that not only is Chris willing to go to the dark side and do the difficult thing, but also that he may have a particular appetite for it as well. Dark-side tactics are useful when a CIO needs simple compliance and obedience, or needs to send a strong message but does not expect or require enthusiasm from others.

CIOs must demonstrate that they have the following dark-side behaviors:

- Use power and negative incentives deliberately when needed to create compliance
- Demonstrate the ability to make ethical and value trade-offs when there is no win-win
- Protect territory and followers, punish potential threats and expand territory as needed
- Avoid battles when possible by being powerful, frightening and manipulating opponents

- Take calculated rather than reckless risks, and deal with large-scale and evolving attacks
- Aspire to be viewed as a leader to be taken seriously and worthy of a strong alliance

When CIOs engage in these behaviors, they are viewed as strong and formidable. Staff and colleagues respect them and will follow them because they know these CIOs can get things done and can provide for them as well as protect them. As a result, they feel safe as part of the community. They know that the CIO wields his dark powers on behalf of his followers and friends rather than against them. Of course, the caveat is that they are only protected as long as they are loyal to the CIO.

Few leadership guides focus on the dark side of leadership as Machiavelli did in his works. This is often because of a false assumption that such tactics are unwarranted or destructive and only serve the leader. And in fact, when a leader uses dark-side tactics exclusively, he may eventually be viewed as self-serving or too powerful and frightening to continue to exist. But, when leaders use dark-side tactics appropriately on behalf of their teams and their enterprises, they become strong protectors, effective champions for their causes, and able to care for and nurture what they have built.

The Wolf's answer is never one or the other; it is always both

Some of the most common leadership questions include whether it is better to be liked or respected, to be loved or feared, or to be admired or loathed? Machiavelli's works and CIO experiences would suggest that these are not simple binary choices. Although we would like to believe that we have the luxury, or perhaps even a societal mandate, to choose to be on the light side exclusively, in reality a leader must choose to master both sides of the binary equation if she hopes to be successful. Being liked is tremendously helpful, particularly when things are going wrong, as often this affection is the only thing that may win a CIO another chance to succeed. When being admired fails, which it sometimes does, it is useful to be loathed. Only by exploring the extremes of light and dark can a CIO grow his strength, and mature into a fully grown, grey Machiavellian Wolf.

Wolf Packet

By reading this far you are now an honorary member of the Wolf Pack. Becoming a full-fledged Wolf CIO is a journey. To help you with your journey, at the end of each step you will find a "Wolf Packet" of items to remember and take with you on the next part of the journey. Like a sugar packet, the Wolf Packets are compact, self-contained and intended to help fuel your next steps. But as we are dealing with challenging light- and dark- side issues throughout our journey, be aware that these packets may often taste bittersweet.

Remember:

- Extreme situations require animal inspiration
- Don't bring data to a knife fight
- What animal would you use to describe yourself?
- Wolf CIOs are both grey and binary
- The light side of the Wolf inspires loyalty
- When IT initiatives require creativity and inspiration, go to the light side
- The dark side of the Wolf inspires fear
- When you need simple compliance and obedience, go to the dark side
- The Wolf's answer is never one side or the other; it is always both

2: Master the Three Essential Machiavellian Wolf Disciplines: Power, Manipulation and Warfare

Men generally decide upon a middle course, which is most hazardous; for they know neither how to be entirely good or entirely bad.

Machiavelli, The Discourses

Practice does make perfect; go to extremes with skill

As Machiavelli noted, many leaders choose a middle course of action because they do not really know how to be entirely good or entirely bad. Although most individuals strive to be good, it is not always clear what that means. Consider the number of times in a given day you ask yourself, *Am I doing the right thing?* For most, this question arises continuously around both personal and professional matters. Questioning and doubt are ethically healthy. Individuals who have no moral doubt are a matter of concern, as this may indicate a personality beyond extreme and best described as radical.

CIOs are no different from anyone else in how they deal with good and bad. They have healthy doubts.

While in my experience the vast majority of CIOs aspire to be quite good, it is not always clear what this means. When being good doesn't work, they sometimes compromise their principles and practices, and end up dissatisfied both with the middle-ground results and with themselves. In too many cases they then go to an opposite extreme at the worst possible time, either accidentally or recklessly.

You may be in this situation if you recently thought or said any of these things: *This used to be such a nice place to work, I don't like being here anymore, nothing seems to work, I'm going to quit, this just isn't worth it, but you know before I go I'm going to write an email to the board telling them how messed up everything is around here and how they don't have a clue either about technology or how to run this business, that will show them!*

If you are feeling this way, your normal management tools and tactics may no longer be working, and you may have inadvertently moved into self-destructive or reckless mode. This is not the time to use extreme tactics. Consider Joseph, a CIO for a large European plastics firm. I helped him prepare his board presentation to outline his IT strategy going forward. We created a presentation designed to excite the board around Joseph's innovative ideas to help the business grow.

A few months later, Joseph told me with a smile that I got him fired and thanked me. What happened? The presentation went exceptionally well and the board enthusiastically engaged Joseph after the meeting. But what Joseph hadn't told me was that his CEO did not appreciate it when anyone outshone him at board meetings or other executive forums. He expressed his displeasure to Joseph, and soon thereafter fired him. It turned out that Joseph really wanted to be fired in this manner to help the board understand the truth about the self-serving CEO. So Joseph used my advice to help him leave his job with a big splash.

Although there are some admirable Machiavellian elements to Joseph's tactics, and going to extremes may be necessary and understandable in unhappy situations such as this, it's preferable to use extreme behaviors deliberately to change your situation for the better, rather than as a way of creating a goodbye trail of career wreckage. Joseph might have considered, for example, confiding in a trusted board member and gaining his advice, or alerting the Chief Legal Officer that the CEO may be a liability. Joseph may have done all this and more, and resorted to getting himself fired having exhausted all other options. CIOs must practice a variety of extreme tactics to gain the skills they need to become strong Wolf CIOs and gain the ability to use these tactics to prevent negative situations from getting out of control.

Leaders must master the disciplines of power, manipulation and warfare

Machiavelli wrote three major political works that advised on the primary disciplines he believed mattered most to leadership excellence. His three works inspire the major themes and sections of this work: *The Prince*, *The Discourses* and *The Art of War*. Each of these works is relevant to CIOs today.

The first and most popular of his writings, *The Prince*, is essentially a guidebook on how to be a powerful dictator. During Machiavelli's time, Italy did not exist as a political construct; the peninsula was a collection of independent regions led by dukes (i.e., dictators) who periodically went to war, formed alliances and then went to war again. Many of the lessons of The Prince focus on gaining and retaining power. CEOs tend to like this book, so CIOs should, at a minimum, be aware of its lessons so that they can better understand what their CEOs are doing to them, and ideally, apply its tactics to enhance their success.

The second Machiavellian work, *The Discourses*, explores his preferred form of government, a Republic where power is divided among the many rather than the few. This model can prevent the excesses that often come with dictatorships; however, leading in such an environment is complex. Many players are continuously maneuvering for position and territory. They alternate between competing with one another and collaborating, and between self-interest and the greater good. This environment best resembles that of a modern corporation or government, and the skills associated with leading effectively require not only power but intelligence and calculation, otherwise known as manipulation. When they set their minds to it, CIOs have tremendous potential to master this particular discipline given their existing data-driven skill set.

The third political work, Machiavelli's treatises that make up *The Art of War*, explored the qualities of a great General and included detailed descriptions of early military maneuvers. Growing revenues, centralization, consolidations, cost cutting and other common business projects are often hostile activities that face resistance and require long-term planning, organization and adaptability resembling those associated with planning a military campaign. Whether or not they care to, most CIOs must manage conflict, sometimes on multiple fronts, and it is too late to prepare if the enemy is already gunning for you.

Power, manipulation and warfare are extreme disciplines. Each has an extreme light side and an extreme dark side. By learning the skills associated with them over time, a CIO can develop a calm and controlled approach to even the most stressful situations. Stress and extreme reactions such as, *I'm going to quit*, often result from the frustration of not knowing what to do or being in a situation one has not encountered before. While no leader will succeed in every hostile situation, mastering these disciplines will increase your success rate, and perhaps more importantly, decrease your stress over time.

Go to animal extremes to strengthen your inner Wolf

Becoming a Wolf CIO is not a linear path; rather it involves continuously moving from one end of the three extreme Machiavellian disciplines to the other — from the light side to the dark side and back again. CIOs must demonstrate that they are able to go to extremes so that colleagues, staff and stakeholders know they are capable of them. Once a CIO demonstrates that she is capable of a variety of extreme behaviors, she will be perceived as strong and capable. Then, a CIO needs to apply extreme behaviors less frequently, as periodic reminders that she is still strong and capable of them, or as needed in a specific situation. As one CIO put it, "If you have a weapon, you have to use it. Otherwise, everyone will think that either the weapon doesn't work, or you don't have the nerve to use it." After establishing the working condition of the weapon and your willingness to use it, later you simply have to show it to achieve the desired effect.

At the most extreme ends of the spectrum, the CIO behaviors associated with power, manipulation and warfare look less Wolf-like, and more like those of more radical animals. The Extreme Animal Ecosystem illustrates these behaviors to help you develop your inner Wolf.

Extreme Animal Ecosystem

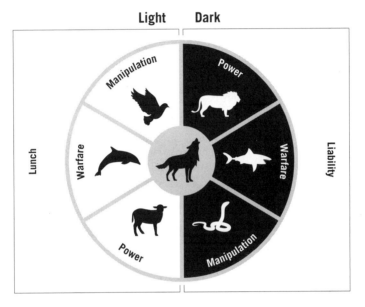

The ecosystem shows six extreme animals at the edges, with the Wolf in the center. Each animal represents a set of Machiavellian-inspired behaviors that CIOs can develop as part of their leadership toolkit. Half of the animals are on the light side of the leadership tactics — the Lamb, Dove and Dolphin. The other half are on the dark side of the leadership tactics — the Lion, Snake and Shark. Like a hub-and-spoke model, the Wolf is in the center. To develop the Wolf, you have to strategically move to the extremes and master the tactics best associated with each of the extreme animals. The Wolf is at full strength when it has gained the essence of all six of the other animals.

The animals are also paired to represent the binary light and dark extremes of each of the three disciplines. The Lamb and Lion represent binary power extremes, where the Lamb is low in overt power but has other leadership strengths, while the Lion has great overt power but is weak in other power tools. The Dove and Snake represent manipulation extremes, where the Dove is unlikely to manipulate covertly and use virtue as its primary weapon, while the Snake is highly manipulative and stealthy, but may be too adaptable in its ethics to be trustworthy. The Dolphin represents the need for a CIO to be highly social and charismatic at one end of the spectrum, while at the other end, the Shark can dispatch threats with extreme prejudice. The remaining sections of this book detail what CIO behaviors look like at each of these extremes, when to apply them and when to avoid them.

In each of the three disciplines, the Wolf represents a strongly balanced center point at which the light and dark extremes are moderated and the positive and negative aspects of each discipline are combined appropriately. Many Wolf tactics are blends of both light and dark, and thus are best described as grey.

Extreme Animal Ecosystem principles:

- You may find that you resemble one of the six extreme animals more than you do the Wolf. This is ok — knowing your starting point or dominant leadership style is an important part of the journey to expanding your toolkit. Consider taking the online diagnostic available at www.gartner.com/wolfcio to find your starting point and track your progress over time.

- When CIOs spend too much time on the light side of the behavioral ecosystem, they may be perceived as good, but weak, and risk becoming the equivalent of prey or "lunch" if their colleagues or the enterprise culture tends toward the dark side.

- When CIOs spend too much time on the dark side of the behavioral ecosystem, they risk being perceived as bad and self-serving, and may become tagged as a liability that must be eliminated, especially if the enterprise culture tends toward the light side.

- Without the Wolf in the middle, the CIO has only extreme behaviors. Such leaders may appear volatile, insensitive, overreacting or addicted to drama, and will wear out their welcome in even the most patient enterprise after a while.

- A Wolf embodies all six of the extreme animals at the same time. And while a Wolf can and will go to the binary extremes of light and dark, having a blend of both sets of skills and tactics ensures that neither one side nor the other goes out of balance, or is perceived as going out of balance.

A Wolf without the extremes is just a dog

Most importantly, CIOs should note that without the extreme behaviors, a Wolf is just a dog. Dogs are wonderful creatures that have been bred from wolves over the centuries, but breeding has eliminated all of the more extreme traits of the species. This makes a dog a safer pet than a wolf, but a CIO should never be domesticated. The unfortunate challenge is that some enterprises figuratively cage their CIOs, limiting their resources and relegating them to doing what they are told, then wonder why they don't have a competitive killer in the technology arena. In some cases, CIOs inadvertently cage themselves by limiting their tactics and perspective. Fortunately, both of these situations are fixable.

The journey to Wolf is not a linear one from the light side to grey moderation. In dark-side enterprises, CIOs who start on the light side are often perceived as weak. When they become grey, they may be perceived as weak leaders who are trying to be perceived as strong by taking the middle ground. Instead, CIOs must go to dark extremes because then, when they return to the grey Wolf center, they are perceived as extremely strong leaders who are actually restraining themselves by being moderate, and thus magnanimous.

As Machiavelli noted, there is no safe middle ground in leadership. Practicing only "safe" middle-ground leadership behaviors weakens a CIO because others will become convinced that there is nothing extraordinary or remarkable about you. So dare to explore the less-safe extremes, and dare to become remarkable.

You come from the light side, so we're going into the dark

Based on my experience, the majority of CIOs spend most of their time on the light side of the ecosystem. This is admirable and appropriate so long as your enterprise has a light-side culture. Many leadership books provide advice to CIOs and other executives about the use of light-side tactics, based on the assumption they are dealing with a culture that is also light or open to light-side tactics.

But most CIOs come to me when their light-side tactics are no longer working because they find themselves in a weak position, have entered a new CIO role where the environment is hostile, or they have new executive leadership and a culture that is either dark or dysfunctional, or all of the above. Therefore, much of what follows will focus on why light-side tactics do not work in dark-side cultures, and how to apply extreme dark-side or grey Wolf tactics to succeed in these environments.

You, the good guy or gal, can still win, but you will have to go to the dark side to do it.

Wolf Packet

Remember:

- Practice does make perfect; go to extremes with skill
- Leaders must master the disciplines of power, manipulation and warfare
- Go to animal extremes to strengthen your inner Wolf
- Half of the animals are on the light side of the leadership tactics — the Lamb, Dove and Dolphin. The other half are on the dark side of the leadership tactics — the Lion, Snake and Shark. Like a hub-and-spoke model, the Wolf is in the center

- The animals are also binary pairs, with the Lamb and Lion representing power, the Dove and Snake representing manipulation, and the Dolphin and Shark representing warfare
- A Wolf without the extremes is just a dog
- You come from the light side, so we're going into the dark

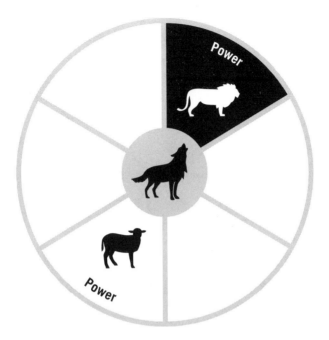

Section I: Power

Great men experienced great difficulties in their course, and met danger at every step, which could only be overcome by their courage and ability.

But once having surmounted them, then they began to be held in veneration; And having crushed those who were jealous of their great qualities, they remained powerful, secure, honored, and happy.

Machiavelli, *The Prince*

3: Recognize the Power You Have and Increase It Exponentially

He who does not lay the foundations for his power beforehand may be able by great ability and courage to do so afterward;

But it will be done with great trouble to the builder and with danger to the edifice.

Machiavelli, *The Prince*

Treat power as an ethically neutral construct

According to Machiavelli, it is better to plan ahead to gain power so that you have it in store in case you need it, rather than try to amass it when you may be under attack. Otherwise, while it may be possible to use power, it will be much more difficult. Many leadership books claim to examine the concept of a strong leader or executive; however, few directly confront the issue of power. Power and strong leadership are inseparable.

Although many leaders mistakenly view power as inherently negative, Machiavelli treated it as an essential tool. We have all been warned that power corrupts. However, strong leadership requires a thoughtful and constructive relationship with power. Power comes in many forms ranging from coercion to credibility, and its use cannot be reduced to a simple question of extreme avoidance versus dictatorial abuse. Each form of power has both a light and a dark side, for the one who wields the power and for those on the receiving end.

Power is an ethically neutral construct that CIOs can use for good or ill. CIOs without power cannot use it to benefit themselves, their subordinates or the enterprise. While no one appreciates having power used against them, it is equally true that no one enjoys working for a leader they perceive as weak or ineffectual. As leaders, CIOs must understand power in all its complexity and know how and when to wield power for maximum effect.

The word "power" evokes strong emotions and biases; therefore, defining power is important. Basically, power is the ability to make something happen — an attribute we expect in all leaders. Methods of achieving power may be good or bad, but looking to make something happen is an ethically neutral expectation.

"Politics" is another emotionally charged word that many people avoid defining, or that they define only to the extent that it is something they never engage in. For our purposes, politics is simply the process of resolving conflicts and making decisions. All leaders must be able to resolve contentious issues. Although we may aspire to have a conflict-free environment with clear decision roles and a supportive culture that works collaboratively toward goals shared by all, few of us have the luxury of such a workplace.

To master power, as with any complex skill, a leader must first embrace it unapologetically and recognize that wielding it is both an opportunity and a threat. CIOs should approach the opportunity with enthusiasm for the good they can do once they gain power, and approach the threat of the damage power can do with the respect it deserves.

Use the ubiquitous nature of IT to become more powerful rather than vulnerable

The ubiquitous nature of IT makes a CIO at once powerful and vulnerable. As a public-sector CIO explained, "Everyone depends on IT every minute of every day. If a system goes down for a minute, people know it, whereas the work of a CFO or HR executive, if less than their best effort, probably won't be evident at first, maybe for quite some time and possibly never."

The vulnerability aspect of this dynamic subjects CIOs to a level of scrutiny and criticism their peers may never experience. Consider the outlandishness of an entire enterprise reviewing the CFO's and CEO's work every day and regularly offering critiques. This might be beneficial, but these executives, for the most part, escape such scrutiny. CIOs and IT departments, however, can neither opt out of their intimate relationships with users nor entirely eliminate the risks associated with this kind of exposure.

How does the ubiquitous nature of IT make CIOs powerful? A CIO in the financial services sector observed, "When I am successful, everyone can see and it greatly increases my credibility." And a manufacturing CIO noted, "No one can do a project of any significant size without me. Almost all such projects involve some kind of IT. I can give them resources or not, so it is in their best interest to work collaboratively with me. Otherwise, I'm not likely to provide scarce resources to them."

IT can generate growth, reduce the cost of doing business and mitigate business risks, the things that all executives care about most. Each time a CIO delivers these benefits to the enterprise, it is an opportunity to grow power.

But power is not solely about performance. It is also about belief and perception. Unfortunately, too many CIOs focus on vulnerability at the expense of empowerment. This may be because IT executives view the use of power differently from their peers. This stems in part from the perception of IT as a service provider, which places the organization in a powerless and reactive mode. Shifting the power-vulnerability dynamic in favor of power requires changing this self-perception, as well as behavioral patterns and skill sets, by using extreme measures.

Extreme Animal Ecosystem: Binary Power Animals

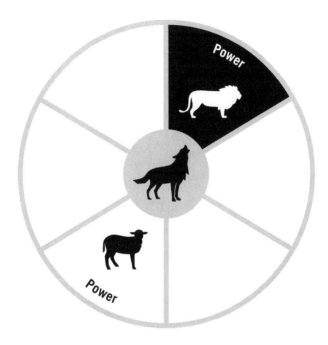

Wolves are powerful creatures. As discussed earlier, developing similar power as a leader involves going to extremes of light and dark. The Lamb on the light side of power, and the Lion on the dark side best symbolize the power extremes. Are you more of a Lamb or a Lion?

Lamb CIOs strive to be liked and to please others

CIOs with a Lamb power approach are often driven by a desire to be liked and likeable. They enjoy having a positive working environment, and generally prefer not to stand out either positively or negatively. Many may view them as having an affable lack of ego because they tend not to be concerned with power or status. They exhibit some of the following characteristics:

- Others work with them because they like them or want to protect them
- Are reluctant to say no as they want to please others
- Use positive incentives to motivate staff but are reluctant or unable to discipline
- Viewed as good leaders in good times, and very good followers, but not fighters

CIOs with these characteristics tend to rise to power in collegial cultures or when a leader with an extremely negative style needs to be replaced. There is tremendous power in being liked. The tendency of others to protect Lamb-like leaders can curb the more aggressive tendencies of other leaders. There are negative implications as well. These CIOs in the extreme are conflict-avoidant, and will often fail to develop conflict management skills. If the leadership or competitive environment turns hostile, they are often not viewed as the fighter to take the enterprise to the next level. So they may be let go or relegated to a different position where they may run a more "steady state" part of IT or the business.

All CIOs must be able to put on this sheep's clothing when need be and take on the behaviors and characteristics of a Lamb. Even the strongest CIOs have stronger adversaries. For example, the CEO often overrules everyone in the enterprise so only rarely can a CIO hope to overpower one. In such situations, it can be expedient to behave as a Lamb until other tactics become effective, a point we'll discuss more in subsequent chapters.

Lion CIOs strive to be strong and able to execute

CIOs with a Lion approach actively gather positional and coercive power. They are aware of the power that comes with their positions and actively exercise that power like a muscle in the interest of growing it and gaining more territory. When needed, they will use coercive power or status to get cooperation from those who would not agree to participate otherwise. They are very sensitive to the relationship between perception and reality and "roar" a lot to communicate what they have accomplished. Others want to work with them because they can get things done. They also exhibit some of the following characteristics:

- Others admire them and want to be associated with or gain their protection
- Gains power by managing up the hierarchy, gaining positional power, authority and status

- Confidence and charisma are high, but may fail to listen or get input when needed
- Viewed as good at execution, but not as inspirational, strategic or good followers

CIOs with this style often rise to power in cultures that are more aggressive or internally competitive since they can hold their own with other "predators." They can often rise quickly in organizations as they exhibit many traits classically associated with leadership and "managing up." These CIOs, however, are often viewed not as inspirational leaders but as "the muscle" that enforces unpopular technology decisions through mandates and authority. In the extreme, others may have no motivation other than coercion to follow them. So if the formal power shifts, as may happen if a more collaborative CEO enters the scene, these CIOs are often left without any other tools to get the job done and may leave the organization very quickly thereafter.

A Wolf is neither Lamb nor Lion, but both

In the center is the inspirational yet strong Wolf CIO who knows when to be a Lion and when to be a Lamb, and blends the light and the dark side into grey strategies to help her succeed. CIOs face specific situations when their power may be enhanced or drained. These situations range from handling pet project requests from stakeholders to handling control issues, and dealing with power vacuums. To understand how to implement light- and dark-side extremes and create a more balanced grey, the remaining chapters in this section will describe how individual CIOs have employed animal tactics in their roles. Let's begin with one of the most critical and revealing power conundrums — dealing with more demands for IT than you can possibly handle. Are you a Lamb, a Lion or well on your way to being a Wolf CIO?

Wolf Packet

Remember:

- Treat power as an ethically neutral construct
- Strong leadership requires a thoughtful and constructive relationship with power
- Use the ubiquitous nature of IT to become more powerful rather than vulnerable
- Lamb CIOs strive to be liked and to please others
- CIOs with Lamb characteristics tend to rise to power in collegial cultures or after a leader with an extremely negative style is replaced
- Lion CIOs strive to be strong and able to execute
- CIOs with Lion characteristics often rise to power in cultures that are more aggressive or internally competitive since they can hold their own with other "predators"
- Even the strongest CIOs have stronger adversaries
- A Wolf is neither Lamb nor Lion, but both

4: Prioritize With Force and Finesse

Hate is gained as much by good works as by evil.

Machiavelli, *The Prince*

If you have the ability to say no, say no

Doug, the CIO of a large local government law enforcement agency, entered the organization over a year ago, and discovered a project list with more than 400 projects. Some of the project requests had been placed almost three years prior to his arrival. Doug had no idea how many of the project requests were still valid, or how important any of them really were.

Prioritization had been left to the IT team, who picked the projects they wanted to work on, those they felt were doable or those that belonged to the stakeholders who screamed the loudest. Agency leadership had come to despise IT, viewing the team as unresponsive, opaque and accomplishing very little. In an attempt to change the situation, Doug asked to convene a governance group to help deal with prioritization, and the key stakeholders refused. In this dark-side culture, stakeholders preferred to avoid accountability and did not have a strong sense of teamwork.

What would you do or have you done in this increasingly common situation? Virtually all CIOs today face the reality of having much more demand for IT than they can possibly deliver with the resources they have available. Machiavelli warned that hate emanates from good works and good intentions as well as from evil. Whether a leader cooperates with a long list of demands or finds other ways of dealing with them is a significant factor in determining his real and perceived power level in the enterprise.

Many CIOs take the Lamb power approach to prioritization. They hope to please others and avoid conflict by saying yes to as many projects as possible and end up with many more projects than they can possibly fulfill. When colleagues decline to participate in prioritization, light-side CIOs may even make kindly excuses for them such as, *They are very busy running the business and don't have time to prioritize, so we'll just do the best we can.* They are often surprised when their colleagues fail to appreciate their well-intentioned efforts. In the extreme, their cooperation is met with contempt. While colleagues may appreciate a CIO's efforts for a while, over time they will move to the dark side and grow to view a CIO's inability to say no not as a sign of willingness to help or a positive attitude, but rather as a sign of weakness. A stronger stakeholder believes that, *If the CIO had the power to say no, then of course he would say no.*

Avoid giving your power to others who will not use it wisely

Paul is the CIO of an aerospace company. In a similar situation, he convenes a governance group, tells them how much money and resource is available for IT, asks them to pare down the projects and commits to IT delivering what they choose. Unfortunately for Paul, they do not choose anything resembling infrastructure or replacement of legacy systems. Nothing builds on or optimizes a previously existing system.

Virtually everything they choose is a new "shiny object" his team is unfamiliar with, and which will add complexity to their overall system architecture. A "shiny object" in executive parlance, is something that's new, cool, makes pretty colors, and is preferably better and "shinier" than what the other senior executives have. There is generally an inverse relationship between business value and the relative shininess of the object.

Unfortunately, Paul gave away his power to the governance group by letting them make all the decisions. He had adopted the risk approach best known as "plausible deniability." He believes that since his stakeholders made all the choices, they will not blame him when costs skyrocket, delivery falls behind schedule and legacy systems fail. He is mistaken. In a dark-side culture, when the inevitable happens, they will default to self-preservation and blame him by saying things like, *He should have known better than to let us make all the decisions. It's not as though we know anything about IT. He should have told us that other projects were more important. I'll bet it's really just an IT issue.*

Apply a firm paw to guide prioritization decisions

On the other hand, Robert, a Lion CIO for an international group of sports teams, does engage the various teams in the decision making; however, he meets with each team owner individually before he convenes any governance meeting. As Robert describes, "I don't call a governance meeting until I know exactly how everyone is going to vote." He steers the decision making in the individual meetings, moving owners toward some projects that would be good investments and away from others that are not a good fit for the existing architecture or where the potential value is low. As the year goes on, he swaps new projects in and older projects out if the value of the project warrants it.

This strategy is sound and effective, as long as Robert is comfortable with the visibility that comes with the Lion approach. It is quite clear to all of the owners that Robert is leading in this situation, and as such they hold him accountable for the results in a very direct fashion. In the quest to feed the appetite for more value, the constant change in the project list also ensures a continuous stream of potential conflicts, which Robert must monitor and manage. When things go wrong, which they always do since this is IT, all eyes are squarely on Robert's shiny mane. So long as Robert delivers and continues to maintain his power, he is well positioned to succeed.

The Wolf combines force and finesse to benefit the enterprise

We began this chapter with Doug, the government CIO who attempted to engage his stakeholders in prioritizing the bloated and outdated project list of 400 projects. Fortunately for his organization, Doug is a Wolf CIO. When the stakeholders refused to engage, Doug took matters into his own hands. He slashed back the list of 400 projects to 50 of his choosing. He took special care to kill the pet projects of high-priority stakeholders, and then presented the project list to the organization as a fait accompli.

Some objected to his Lion-like dictatorial decision making. "Well," Doug said, "I requested their participation and they deferred to me. Perhaps they should have thought of that before." Others reacted loudly to the elimination of their pet projects. Doug feigned total innocence, noting that "If they had engaged with me, I certainly would have known which projects were important and which were not. Perhaps if they would like to engage now, I could adjust the priority list." By engaging them as a Lamb would and adjusting the project list to please them, Doug learned what the enterprise priorities were, and taught stakeholders the benefits of engaging in a constructive prioritization process.

By combining light and dark tactics, he dealt with the issue at hand and advanced the organization for the better in the long run. Was the process pretty? No. Risky? Yes. Effective? Definitely. But by taking a blended grey Wolf approach, he ensured an optimal outcome for the enterprise and taught his colleagues to take him seriously when he requested their participation, as well as the benefits of being engaged.

Treat pet projects as a power source rather than as a pestilence

Pet projects are a special bone of contention for many CIOs. They can best be defined as projects that are highly important to an individual or group of stakeholders, but provide minimal or dubious business value to the enterprise. Extreme Lambs tend to want to do all of the pet projects in the interest of pleasing everyone. Other Lambs would prefer to eliminate pet projects to save scarce enterprise resources, but would never actually take action and risk making colleagues unhappy. So they work on them, but they and the IT teams often do so reluctantly and eventually somewhat resentfully. A Lion CIO has the power to eliminate all pet projects and may do so for the good of the enterprise. Alternately, a Lion may also opt to do all of the pet projects of the hierarchy since they are sensitive to managing up.

The extreme "kill all pet projects" approach is useful as a one-time message to the enterprise about the proliferation of such projects and the need to eliminate waste. It is not useful as a persistent practice because it misses an important opportunity for a CIO to gain power. Pet projects are part of the currency of gaining power and should be treated as a grey area, rather than a binary one. When a CIO executes one for a colleague, he has gained currency, and can later request that the colleague reciprocate (which gives the CIO even more power). So saying no to all pet projects is usually an opportunity lost. However, always saying yes is a power drain rather than an increase — it denigrates the political value of pet projects to where they become expected. Wolf CIOs are selective in using pet projects to build currency without devaluing the exchange.

Wolf Packet

Many CIOs will give prioritization power away because they prefer not to be seen as the ones making
all the decisions. They have noticed that stakeholders
don't like it when IT has a great deal of power. CIOs
with this belief should ask themselves if their executive colleagues would respond similarly and give away
their power in the same situation. Additionally, how
will the IT team feel if they do not have decision power
in critical situations? Will it put their ability to succeed
at risk? Machiavelli would suggest that if you must
choose between your colleagues having power and you
having it, you should choose yourself.

Remember:

- If you have the ability to say no, say no
- Avoid giving your power to others who will not use it wisely
- Apply a firm paw to guide prioritization decisions
- The Wolf combines force and finesse to benefit the enterprise
- Treat pet projects as a power source rather than as a pestilence

5: Exude Power by Growling, Rather Than Roaring, Your Reputation

We often see that humility not only is of no service, but is actually hurtful;

Especially when employed toward insolent men, who from jealousy or some other motive have conceived a hatred against you.

Machiavelli, *The Discourses*

Decide the reputation you want to have and do not leave it to chance

What words would the CEO use to describe you and your IT department? Would the CEO use words such as innovative, agile and competitive? Or would he say reliable, cost effective and consistent? Are the words unreliable or unresponsive unfortunate possibilities? And how is a CIO to handle this? One of the most valuable things CIOs have is their reputation and that of their IT department. How CIOs manage their reputations can significantly impact their power levels and ability to execute.

Machiavelli suggests that people are easily influenced by what things seem to be, and often prefer perceptions to the challenging task of determining what is real and what is not. His commentary was an early version of the aphorism "perception is reality." It can take a great deal of work to determine what reality actually is in any given situation. And in the fast-paced work environment we live in, few invest in digging below the surface of a difficult situation, or beyond the messages that are passively coming their way.

CIOs with a Lamb power approach are humble, and often take the approach *I don't like to brag about my accomplishments.* Their humility is admirable, and as many CIOs have shared with me over the years, often the result of their personality, culture or family values. In enterprises with similar light-side cultures, these CIOs tend to do well because their organizations respect this quality in a leader. Unfortunately, this can be a suboptimal approach in a dark-side business culture. Power, as noted earlier, is the ability to make things happen. Humble CIOs often take little or no proactive action to ensure that the enterprise knows that they are making things happen. As such, their reputations are in the hands of others and essentially left to chance.

These CIOs will have the expectation that *When I do good work, others will notice.* While it is arguable others should notice, if Machiavelli is correct, which he is, this is unlikely to happen. What often does happen in these situations is that few will hear of the many IT successes, but many will hear of the few IT failures. The exception becomes the rule and the reputation because the only time colleagues will hear anything about IT will be when things have gone wrong.

It is not your job as the CIO to be objective; it is your job to tell the story

Consider Sheila, a CIO in a media company. On a weekly basis she produces IT status reports to distribute to all of the senior and mid-level managers in the company. First Sheila notes all of the bad news such as server outages, security issues, vendor issues and the help desk resolution statistics. This is followed by what is going right — usually a much shorter list, as Sheila suffers from a healthy amount of humility. She is unclear as to why IT has a poor reputation when she is being so transparent and proactive in her communications.

Sheila explains that her approach is based in the common belief that "It is my job as CIO to be objective." Unfortunately, she is mistaken. It is the CIO's job to tell the story and to advocate for and manage the reputation of her organization. If it is not the CIO's job, then whose job is it? CIOs often believe that if they present the right objective data, then stakeholders will be able to figure out the truth. The reality is, your colleagues rarely think that hard about the material in front of them. Everyone in the enterprise is busy with the full-time job of taking care of themselves and advocating for their own organizations. It is not that they don't care; it is simply that they are busy and pragmatic. And sometimes, they just don't care.

Perception does have to match reality, but not perfectly

CIOs with Lion tendencies often go to the opposite extreme and avoid sharing bad news ever. These CIOs are often perfectionists, which is quite common among people with IT backgrounds. Perfectionism is an excellent trait in IT leaders, as roles with a technical component often require detail orientation. This can, however, be problematic in communications. Some perfectionist CIOs worry that small failures will give the impression that the entire IT shop must somehow be damaged. In many cases these CIOs will also avoid communicating good news, *Because the data is not 100% accurate, it is only 90% and I don't want to be wrong.*

Consider David, a CIO from a manufacturing company who avoids getting bad audits at all costs. He aggressively goes to extremes to ensure that the auditors never hear that anything is less than perfect. IT staff who tend to be brutally honest are told to take the day off when the auditor arrives. David's mantra is *Nothing to see here, all is well and there is nothing to report.* Unfortunately, because such CIOs want to be perceived as strong, they tend to "roar" about successes but are reluctant to show weakness, so few volunteer to help them. David seldom receives help from colleagues or significant additional funding. Because everything is always great there is no need for him to receive any assistance. This cycle essentially tightens the noose around David over time as he gains fewer resources and increases expectations, and the illusion of perfection becomes increasingly difficult to maintain.

Wolf CIOs protect their reputations by growling and not being soft targets

Wolf CIOs build their reputations and their power by proactively communicating about their accomplishments and asking for help to deal with real issues. They also aggressively protect those hard-earned reputations by figuratively chewing up and scattering the body parts of those who attack them. They actively hunt down those who say bad things about IT and work to correct the record. Susan, a Wolf CIO from a European retail company, described a situation where one stakeholder repeatedly blamed IT for his inability to generate reports for senior leadership in a timely fashion. Behind closed doors and out of earshot of IT, the stakeholder claimed that each time he went to run the required reports, the system was down, and therefore it was IT's fault that his group was unable to perform.

When Susan discovered what had been transpiring, she went on the offensive. She ran a series of her own reports documenting the times when the system in question had been down in the past 12 months. The data showed that the system had been down for a total of two minutes in the previous year. Susan shared this data with the senior executive team, and as she noted, "It became quite clear that my colleague was playing games." She did not have to roar or shout, or create drama. The threatening growl of data revealed that IT had done its job.

Susan's tactics combined the light side of the Lamb who strives to do a good job with the dark side of the Lion who rips apart her enemies to create a grey Wolf approach best referred to as "perform and protect." The CIO's controlled offensive maneuver made it clear to the stakeholder and other colleagues that IT would not be an easy target for blame. As a result, the colleague in question quickly learned to move on to other, softer targets and leave the CIO and IT alone. While this tactic risks the collateral damage of making an enemy of the colleague, Machiavelli would note that any colleague who behaves in such a manner was not your friend to lose in the first place.

Wolf Packet

CIOs on average tend to be more introverted than their colleagues in the rest of the business and often express concerns about managing their reputations as a result. It is important to note that sound reputation management is not about roaring all the time, being loud or extroverted. It is about communicating the reputation that you want proactively and clearly, and then defending it when necessary. While total silence regarding one's reputation is not an option, we also become deaf to the other extreme of roaring all the time. A periodic low growl can be much more effective in gaining the attention of other predators and making them feel like prey.

Remember:

- Decide the reputation you want to have and do not leave it to chance
- It is not your job as the CIO to be objective; it is your job to tell the story
- Perception does have to match reality, but not perfectly
- Wolf CIOs protect their reputations by growling and not being soft targets

6: Make Sure No One Is Always in Control but You

A prince who knows no other control but his own will is like a madman, and a people that can do as it pleases will hardly be wise.

Machiavelli, *The Discourses*

No one should always get everything that they want

Sean held a job in the private sector as the head of application development for a bank. His alma mater has now hired him to be the new CIO. Much to Sean's surprise, the university is very inefficient in its use of IT. Each department seems to have its own email and servers, and some have dedicated IT staff. Each also has its own admissions and financial systems. The central IT department is understaffed for the complexity of the environment and is also underfunded.

This situation is a common one for CIOs around the world. Decentralization and local control often seems like a good idea to business units, but IT is often left struggling with the implications of the enterprise's reluctance to limit its choices. Machiavelli advised against the risks of allowing anyone complete control over their environment and choices, likening such individuals to a "madman." Many enterprises insist that their CIOs be service providers, *whose job it is to do everything that we want*. To be clear, most of these enterprises will actually say, *We want IT to do everything that the business needs*. But as Machiavelli points out, when one individual or group having total control can quickly degenerate into the madness of the master-servant relationship that addresses wants rather than needs.

No one likes being controlled, limited or told what to do. It is human nature, and Machiavelli was an astute student of human nature and history. But as he noted, people without boundaries tend to behave very, very badly. This is especially true when it comes to technology. IT represents, quite literally, shiny objects that senior executives sometimes pursue as though in pursuit of new toys. Set a child loose in a toy store and pandemonium is sure to ensue. Expect screaming, crying and tantrums if they don't get what they want when they want it. Set a pack of executives loose in a virtual IT shop and expect the same result. The tantrums are the same, but the toys are much more expensive. CIOs must exercise power over the potential IT pandemonium for the good of the entire enterprise.

Asking for input or permission in excess equals giving away your power

Sean is a Lamb CIO who opted not to attempt to control the chaos at all. He was new to the CIO role and somewhat awed by being part of the university staff he held in high esteem. So he chose to trust their wisdom once again and tried his best to deliver the complexity they requested. *They always seemed to know what they were talking about before, so they must know now, right?* Wrong. Unfortunately, with limited resources, Sean soon found himself struggling to keep up. When he attempted to suggest some control and standards, his stakeholders assured him that they knew better and he simply didn't understand "The University Way" and how things worked yet. Over time, his stakeholders viewed his failure to deliver as an indication they had chosen the wrong CIO rather than the wrong approach to IT. After just a year, Sean left and returned to private industry. It was an unfortunate and unnecessary loss for both the university and Sean.

Similarly, other CIOs such as Charles, from a multinational professional services provider, standardize only what they can convince their stakeholders to let them control. He worked with key stakeholders to convince them of the positive business case around standardizing a highly decentralized set of systems, particularly from a cost and security perspective. Given the culture and skills of the stakeholders, they were not easily convinced, and gaining initial agreement took months. Solidifying an approach took many more months. In the meantime, the enterprise was over-spending on IT and leaving itself vulnerable to critical security and compliance issues.

While gaining support is generally a prudent approach in a light-side culture, Charles should have asked himself why he wanted the support. There are only two reasons for a CIO or anyone else to solicit the input of stakeholders — either the stakeholder has information that will improve the quality of the IT decision or the CIO requires permission to make a change he does not have the power to make independently. Neither of these was the case in Charles's situation. Charles wanted their input primarily because he believed that proceeding democratically was the fairest way to approach the issue.

Unfortunately, democracy by definition disperses power among the populace and away from the leader. By engaging stakeholders so extensively and essentially asking their permission for each move he made, Charles effectively gave away all his power to the unruly masses. CIOs must distinguish between information gathering and asking permission. Gathering a reasonable amount of input when it is needed is wise. Allowing others to make decisions democratically when it is not required can create a massive control and power drain.

Lions are comfortable with control, but sometimes too comfortable

Lion CIOs allow their stakeholders minimal input and will often exercise control through their positional power alone. Maria, a CIO for a South American gaming company that ran online gambling operations, was such a CIO. When Maria arrived at the company, multiple executives were making IT purchases with no central coordination. Maria made the argument to the CEO and Chief Legal Officer that she could not guarantee that they would be compliant with the myriad regulations that they were subject to without her having more direct control over the IT. The CEO and CLO agreed, with the condition that as long as Maria executed well, she would retain control over the decisions.

Maria had successfully gained control and successfully functioned well as the CIO for several years. Unfortunately, over time, Maria lost perspective, control of herself and of the situation. She became arrogant and rarely requested input from stakeholders. When they provided it to her anyway, she rarely listened; she had grown overly confident in her ability to make the right decisions. Then, IT experienced a moderate failure that affected the online gaming systems and resulted in revenue losses. The CEO almost immediately fired Maria. In utilizing extreme control and dark-side power tactics exclusively, Maria had become the mad leader that Machiavelli warned about, and was eliminated when the opportunity presented itself.

Wolves calculate the risk of deliberately not doing what they are told

Consider Russell, a Wolf CIO who joined a highly decentralized university in the southern United States with no standardized approaches. He asked permission of all of the university presidents to standardize IT infrastructure and email to save money and improve security. Preferring to keep control themselves, they predictably and collectively said "no." What was the CIO's reaction to the rebuff? According to Russell, "I standardized anyway and they didn't notice." Essentially, each time a system required significant new capability or substantial maintenance or upgrading, Russell would quietly move it to a more standardized system and consulted no one outside of the IT team. IT was enthused about moving away from the older, unmanageable systems and was thus motivated to keep these behaviors to themselves.

This approach is not for the risk-averse CIO. Russell the Wolf, however, was not reckless. His combined light- and dark-side approach is the grey tactic of *give them what they need, even if they don't want it.* He calculated the risk of irritating stakeholders who had given him poor guidance due to their lack of familiarity with IT against the risk that they would blame him anyway when the complex systems failed. He always delivered the capabilities that they needed, just not necessarily in the suboptimal manner they requested. If they noticed what he had done, he was convinced he could better argue his case after the fact through the strong results he delivered. Russell had usurped power from the masses without their knowledge, seizing it over their objection. But he did so in a controlled and calculated manner that maximized the benefit for IT and the enterprise, while minimizing the risk for both at the same time.

Wolf Packet

Remember:

- No one should always get everything that they want
- Asking for input or permission in excess equals giving away your power
- Lions are comfortable with control, but sometimes too comfortable
- Wolves calculate the risk of deliberately not doing what they are told

7: Follow the Money but Don't Let It Fool You

Money alone, so far from being a means of defense, will only render a prince the more liable to being plundered.

There cannot, therefore, be a more erroneous opinion than that money is the sinews of war.

Machiavelli, *The Discourses*

Having money makes a CIO both powerful and vulnerable

Money is power. There is no avoiding the reality that the degree of a CIO's control over budget money often determines how difficult their ability to execute will be. The ability to move money and strategically invest it is fundamental to the CIO's ability to create change. But as Machiavelli points out, money does not always ensure strength and safety. Having control of large sums of money can make a CIO powerful and help ensure better IT decision making. It also makes CIOs and IT a significant target of attack, as others covet the funds for alternate uses. When resources become scarce due to a revenue drain or other change in market conditions, competition for money inside the enterprise can quickly turn a light culture to the dark side.

Seth was a CIO with a Lamb approach to power. His enterprise manufactures steel and other metal products multinationally. Seth decided to charge back to the business units for corporate IT infrastructure and enterprise applications. At the same time, he also allowed independent business units to have their own local IT staffs and IT implementations as long as they followed corporate IT policies and architectural guidelines. This is a common approach among CIOs globally, which provides a seemingly balanced approach with federated control over the total IT budget. Seth employed this approach because he believed its transparent and inclusive nature would lead to few conflicts over how the money was being spent. Unfortunately, this approach can inadvertently ensure a battle between corporate and business-unit IT departments when resources become scarce.

When the company's revenue sank because of economic instability in several of their markets, all of the business units began looking for opportunities to save money. The substantial IT budget became a target. Because of the chargeback situation, the now-hostile business-unit IT departments declared that corporate IT was a service provider to them, and they were now the customers. Business-unit IT groups began referring to themselves as "customers" of corporate IT. The business-unit teams began to argue with Seth over the amount of their chargebacks, and the value they received for the money. Seth spent many hours of valuable time documenting and justifying the chargeback costs. He tried to convince his colleagues that they should switch the conversation to how to use IT to help grow the business, but being already agitated, they saw this as a diversionary tactic. The chargeback discussions had become a major distraction.

You may be paying, but that doesn't mean you have the power

In Seth's situation, one of the Machiavellian elements he failed to realize was that in this situation, he actually had the ability to take the Lion power approach rather than the Lamb. Consider that the behavioral dynamic stemmed from the business units' belief that because they were paying a chargeback, they had all the power and could force Seth to present dozens of pages and many hours of justifications of their charges. Seth, on some level, had accepted this premise and complied as someone with a Lamb power level would. But what if their premise about the power dynamic was wrong?

In Seth's case, the university financial system required the business units to pay the chargeback whether or not they felt the quality of the "service" was up to their standards. The charge was made automatically, and policy dictated that business units were not permitted to use an external service provider if they were unhappy with the corporate infrastructure and enterprise applications. This is the situation in many enterprises today. Many shared-service centers have been created with a version of this financial model and the players are restricted from going outside the system to ensure economies of scale and cost savings. This may not always save money, but that is why they are designed this way.

When business units have no choice but to pay a chargeback fee, they are not in fact *customers* of corporate IT; rather, they are *hostages*. When a business unit does not have the power to opt out of a chargeback relationship, it does not have the upper hand. Sean failed to realize he had actually had the power. Understandably, Seth wanted his colleagues to be happy. Unfortunately, in a revenue-challenged situation, happiness is an extreme goal. A more realistic goal would be to engage his colleagues appropriately, but only to the point where they would be able to *tolerate the financial system*. CIOs in these situations should opt to go the extreme of halting or minimize the time spent justifying the chargeback fees and refocus everyone's valuable time on helping the business grow. Unfortunately, such conflicts often continue as long as the chargeback system is in place and the power dynamic is misunderstood.

Wolves keep colleagues off balance rather than making them comfortable

Diana is a Wolf CIO. She joined a very old southeast Asian petroleum company with a small and decentralized IT budget. In the long history of the company, there had never been a woman on the senior executive team. Much to her surprise, Diana's initial recommendations regarding centralizing and increasing the IT budget were met with unanimity from the executive team. They quickly approved all of her requests for more staff, more control over the existing budget and more budget itself. Initially, Diana believed that either this was the most genial executive team she had ever met, or that she was much more persuasive than she originally thought she was. Neither premise was correct.

Soon, Diana figured out what was really going on. The all-male executive team was reluctant to appear sexist to their first female executive. None of the senior executives wanted to be the first to say no to her, and therefore they quickly and quietly agreed to everything that she asked. Diana had a choice to make. She could go to the light side and insist that they treat her just like everyone else. Instead, Diana took a grey Wolf approach and seized the opportunity she knew would only come once. She chose to leave them feeling off balance and gathered as much money and resources as she could, before the executive team became more comfortable with her. Diana noted, "I doubled the IT budget and staff while centralizing everything. It took six months before anyone said no to me, but by then all of the heavy lifting was done and we were well on our way to much healthier IT for the company." She enjoyed a long and successful career with the company.

In Diana's case, her gender set the rest of the executive team off balance. In other situations it may be a CIO's newness to the team, their age, ethnicity, hair style or hobbies. Any number of variables may be the cause. A Wolf CIO recognizes that this grey "rock the boat" tactic creates discomfort that can be useful and advantageous. Therefore it is better to soothe the group's distress after some advantage has been gained, rather than before. Being different from a group can make you more powerful, while blending in makes them more comfortable and you less powerful.

Wolf Packet

With money and power, things are almost never as they seem. If your beliefs about the power dynamic were wrong, how would you change your behavior? Consider a situation where a colleague funds an IT-related initiative from his budget, and then wants to make all of the decisions regarding it because it is his money. Many CIOs buy into this power premise. But what if it is not their money? Arguably, it did not come of your colleague's personal bank account. When it comes out of the company's budget it is enterprise money, and "our" money. Everyone in the enterprise has a fiduciary responsibility over enterprise money. If a dark-side enterprise changed its power premises, would it change how you treat the money and each other?

Remember:

- Having money makes a CIO both powerful and vulnerable

- You may be paying, but that doesn't mean you have the power

- What if your premise about the power dynamic is wrong?

- When business units have no choice but to pay a chargeback fee, they are not in fact customers of corporate IT, but rather they are hostages

- Wolves keep colleagues off balance rather than making them comfortable

8: Recognize Stronger Wolves and Know When to Be a Lamb

Princes that are attacked cannot commit a greater error, especially when their assailant greatly exceeds them in power, than to refuse all accommodation.

Machiavelli, *The Discourses*

Sometimes your goal is to successfully choose between bad and worse

Even a Wolf CIO is not always the leader of the pack, or the leader of the most powerful pack in the territory. Power does not exist in a vacuum, and Machiavelli was nothing if not pragmatic. One of the key principles underlying his work was the necessity of understanding one's opponents or potential opponents and how you stand in relation to them. In reality, often a CIO's opponents significantly overpower them simply by their position in the hierarchy, and in other cases because they have amassed more power over time. In these situations, Machiavelli advised that refusing to accommodate the requests of a stronger force can be a grave error. In these situations, a CIO should consider pretending to be a Lamb while engaging in Wolf countermeasures to limit the potential damage.

Consider Jack, a Wolf CIO in a South American tele-communications firm. He is not afraid to use power and assert himself when he thinks it's for the good of the enterprise and appropriate to do so. His CFO, Ron, who wanted an iPad, approached Jack. At the time, the iPad was the latest executive shiny object, but there were significant security challenges with placing enterprise data on the device in the firm's environment. Based on security concerns and the lack of a practical business case, Jack declined his CFO's request for the shiny object.

Unfortunately for Jack, his CFO was also not afraid to use power and applied it in an extremely dark-side manner that surprised him. Jack noticed that none of his IT invoices were being signed off or processed by Ron. He assumed this was simply a fluke, until the situation went on for almost a month and the nonpayment began to be an issue. So Jack approached Ron and asked him what was going on. Ron's response? *Well, you know Jack, I am really, really busy. Perhaps if I had an iPad, I could be more productive, and find time to approve your invoices.* The next day, Ron had an iPad on his desk, and the invoices began moving again.

Jack had calculated the risk of his options and settled on a grey Wolf approach of *tactical retreat*. There was no win-win in this situation, only bad and worse. Other than giving in, he could have gone over the CFO's head to the CEO, but decided it was not worth the minimal expense of the device to risk further damaging the relationship with his CFO. Jack survived the battle, and although his position was weakened, he was not compromised entirely by creating a powerful enemy. While giving in was a bad option, all other options were worse.

A partial win is better than no win at all

One of a CIO's greatest nightmares is having an external service provider form a relationship with a senior executive or member of the board and having undue influence over IT-related decisions. There are guidelines and regulations in different countries intended to prevent this from happening, but it is almost impossible to regulate this situation away. Mike, the CIO for a midsize European consultancy that advised the private education industry, experienced this type of situation. When Mike joined the organization, it was growing with tremendous speed and had outgrown the IT service provider that had been used since the company's inception. The small provider simply could not scale as quickly as the growing consultancy required, and it lacked a range of IT capabilities.

Mike developed a business case to move to a much larger provider and asked the CEO to sign off on the approach. The CEO refused. He kept finding seemingly irrelevant reasons to block the change, or would send Mike back repeatedly to gather more data about small issues in the business case. After many months of this, Mike was mystified. Finally, a staffer confided in Mike what was really going on. The owner of the service provider was married to the CEO's daughter, and the company was his only customer.

An inviolable power rule is *blood is always thicker than water, unless we don't like that relative.* In this case, the CEO loved his daughter and while he knew it was time to change service providers, he was locked into a difficult situation. Mike quietly changed his business case to a multisourced approach where the existing service provider retained some of its business, but a larger vendor would also be engaged going forward. The CEO immediately signed off. Although this compromise approach would fall short in the eyes of many as the empirically right thing to do, Mike's ability to subdue his Wolf and allow his Lamb-like empathy for the CEO's situation to come forward enabled him to find a manageable short-term solution. It pleased the CEO and gave the son-in-law who had served the company well time to find other customers.

Sometimes you really are the sacrificial Lamb

Unfortunately not all situations involving external service providers end as well as the previous example. Donna, the CIO of a large North American manufacturing company, faced a situation where several board members pressured her to outsource the majority of

IT staff and capabilities to a major outsourcing firm. The board's contention was that outsourcing would be cheaper than having the existing in-house staff. Donna produced numerous business cases with various scenarios. In each case, the business case demonstrated that her IT shop was so efficient that outsourcing would be either more expensive or only slightly less expensive than the current model. The outsourcer's math showed significant savings.

Donna recommended bringing in an independent consultant to assess the situation. The board refused. By this time she suspected that something else was going on but was never able to determine what it was. She considered threatening to resign. But she worried that the outsourcing would proceed regardless and that the team she cared about would be at the mercy of the board and outsourcer. So she decided to stay on and negotiate the terms of the outsourcing, ensuring that all of her staff either had a position with the outsourcer or the company, or a reasonable severance package. She ensured that the terms of the contract were as favorable to the company as possible. Then she resigned. It is not easy to take the extreme path of a sacrificial Lamb, but there are good reasons to admire CIOs when they do.

Sometimes the Lamb wins big

Many CIOs are faced with mergers, acquisitions and divestments in which their company is somehow combined with another. This situation often results in having multiple CIOs, and the best strategy for being the last one standing is not always what you think. The most common strategy resembles that of the Lion or the Wolf, where CIOs get close to the existing leadership and convince them that they are the strongest candidate. They focus on their successes, try to provide additional visible successes during the transition period while the companies are integrating and try to come out on top. These strategies can work, but sometimes, the Lamb wins.

There are two dominant Lamb power strategies in these situations. The first is best described as, *Blend in with the herd and hope they don't notice you.* This is one of the rare times that not standing out and mimicking a service provider can work in your favor. Other executives may avoid cutting you, thinking *That IT position seems low power and status so I'm not sure I want to deal with it. The person in the CIO role doesn't seem like a threat, and actually seems kind of nice. With all the other staffing decisions I have to make, that one is probably not worth bothering with at the moment so I'll leave it as is.*

Interestingly, by not engaging in the competitive fray, a Lamb often stumbles into the second tactic best described as *playing hard to get.* In this scenario, a CEO will put an acting CIO into place who he is either unsure of or who doesn't appear to be either a threat or potential problem. The acting CIO takes the role and says, *I don't mind being in the acting role, just so long as we're clear that I don't want the permanent job.* CEOs often find this stance both puzzling and intriguing. *You don't want the job? That's interesting. You must have something better lined up. What do they know about you that I don't know yet? I must find out. No, I can't wait to find out. I insist you take the permanent job!*

Remarkably, I have watched a number of acting CIOs take the playing-hard-to-get stance in total sincerity, truly not wanting the job. They were shocked to find themselves aggressively pursued by their CEOs and practically forced into taking the permanent role. There is tremendous power in standing apart and not desperately needing or wanting something. These CIOs inadvertently communicate a certain quiet strength, which is quite appealing to some executive teams. Not seeking power or status for its own sake, they appear selfless and neutral in conflicts. Dark-side cultures that have grown weary of conflict are often the most open and receptive to such Lambs. They seek to put them in place as a respite from the antagonism and as part of turning to the light side. When this happens, both the enterprise and the Lamb CIO win big.

Wolf Packet

Even the most powerful CIOs don't always win, and perhaps they should not. In reality, the hardest lesson of power is dealing with the situations that you simply cannot win. The strongest leaders sometimes have the most difficulty with the losses. Great Wolf CIOs continue to focus on the good of the enterprise and their colleagues in an attempt to minimize the collateral damage, often at great personal or professional expense.

Remember:

- Sometimes your goal is to successfully choose between bad and worse
- A partial win is better than no win at all
- Sometimes you really are the sacrificial Lamb
- It is not easy to take the extreme path of a sacrificial Lamb, but there are good reasons to admire CIOs when they do
- Sometimes the Lamb wins big by acting as though he doesn't want to win

- Dark-side cultures that have grown weary of conflict are often the most open and receptive to Lambs

To achieve true Wolf CIO status, power is not enough. Raw strength is not sufficient to overcome opponents who are extremely cunning or are willing to use secrecy, dishonesty or other manipulation strategies against you. When one's opponent is manipulative, the power-dependent leader is often uncertain where to strike until it is too late.

Being perceived as manipulative is problematic for CIOs and all leaders; however, actually being manipulative is a necessity. CIOs who are perceived as manipulative simply aren't doing it right. The most skilled manipulators are viewed as helpful, empathetic and, in many cases, as charismatic leaders. In Section Two, we focus on the second major Machiavellian discipline, manipulation, and how CIOs can master the art of using it in their organizations.

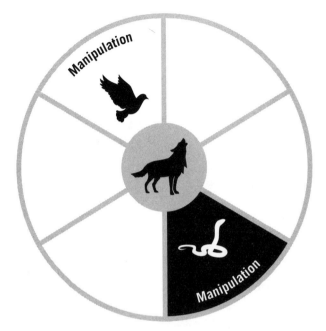

Section II: Manipulation

Faithful servants are always servants, and honest men are always poor;

Nor do any ever escape from servitude but the bold and faithless, or from poverty, but the rapacious and fraudulent.

Hence it is that men feed upon each other, and those who cannot defend themselves must be worried.

Machiavelli, *The History of Florence*

9: Employ Manipulation or Risk Being Manipulated

A prudent ruler ought not to keep faith when by so doing it would be against his interest, and when the reasons which made him bind himself no longer exist.

If men were all good, this precept would not be a good one; but as they are bad, and would not observe their faith with you, so you are not bound to keep faith with them.

Machiavelli, *The Discourses*

Honesty is not the best policy in every situation

Our relationship with the truth and feelings about manipulation are rooted in our beliefs about human nature. If we believe that human beings are basically good, then honesty is the best policy. If we believe they are not, then we might feel differently about honesty. Machiavelli was wrongly imprisoned by the duke he had faithfully served. He was tortured during his three-year imprisonment. This affected his view of the world. He had faith in the duke, and the duke broke his faith with him. Thus Machiavelli learned that assuming that others are basically good can leave you defenseless against them when they are not.

As a CIO, have you ever felt wrongly imprisoned and tortured in IT? Have you ever felt let down by a colleague or perhaps discovered that you had been deliberately misled? Have you ever felt stabbed in the back and surprised that the colleague who did it was someone you thought was your friend? If any of these statements ring true for you, then you may need to become more manipulative. At a minimum, CIOs must learn to recognize manipulation when it is happening to them, and take appropriate countermeasures. Preferably, CIOs must take preventative measures to ensure it does not happen to them, *and* master the art of using manipulation against others.

Manipulation is the dark side of influence

How far would you go to convince someone to do something you felt was best for the enterprise? What would you say to protect your team or an individual you care about from harm? Would you lie, charm, cajole, keep a secret or distract someone from the truth if it was for the greater good? Society sends us mixed messages regarding honesty. Consider how you would answer the question, *Honey, does this outfit make me look fat?* Do you tell the truth, or do you tell the lie? Society sends us mixed messages. *Yes dear, it is much too snug and you're getting a bit wide around the middle. Let's go to lunch. You can have a salad.* This may be the well-intentioned truth, but both society and our partners will punish us for telling it and consider us both thoughtless and lacking in empathy for the feelings of others.

Manipulation takes us deeply into the dark side of human behavior. At its core, manipulation is defined as to handle with skill. Interestingly, the noun management has the same root word and core definition. We tend to be quite comfortable handling objects such as a ball or a tool with skill. We are much less comfortable, as we should be, dealing with the issue of handling people with skill. When we skillfully handle others using light-side techniques, it is often referred to as influence. When we apply dark-side techniques, we are in manipulation territory.

CIOs must overcome practices that make them more likely to be manipulated

When CIOs follow traditional IT management advice and best practices, they often become more vulnerable to the manipulation of others, rather than less vulnerable. Traditional computer science, engineering and management training advises CIOs to be transparent, logical, consistent and goal-driven. Unfortunately, these behaviors can make CIOs predictable to potential manipulators. Manipulators can often countermand CIOs easily because they know exactly what behaviors to expect from them in a given situation and exactly what process they are likely to follow. This predictability can put CIOs at a significant disadvantage when faced with a manipulative adversary.

Machiavelli believed that honesty and transparency are acceptable when one is dealing with a friend. But he warned that when times get tough, or when self-interests override the greater good, then friends can go to the dark side and turn into enemies, and you are left vulnerable. He advised that once someone has broken faith with you by being hostile or deceitful, then it is not only appropriate that you stop being honest with them, but foolhardy to do otherwise. IT leaders, with the best of intentions, often take a one-size-fits-all approach and democratically treat all colleagues the same way, usually as friends. Machiavelli advised that when you treat your friends the same as you do enemies or potential enemies, you place yourself and the enterprise at great risk.

There are three primary situations where manipulation is more appropriate than influence and honesty, and more effective than power: when your colleagues are deceitful, irrational or more powerful than you are. Deceitful colleagues have broken faith in the past and are therefore likely to do so in the future. Irrational stakeholders are impervious to data or traditional reason. And stakeholders who are more powerful than you are will be impervious to your strength level and require alternative tactics. How many of your colleagues display one or more of these characteristics?

Extreme Animal Ecosystem: Binary Manipulation Animals

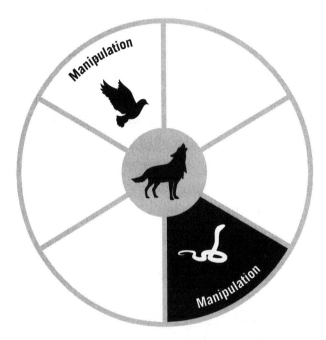

Wolves are intelligent and manipulative creatures. Wolf packs have been known to howl at multiple pitches to fool others into thinking that there are many more wolves in the pack than they appear. They avoid fighting with larger predators, but if one intrudes upon their territory they will rush the intruder and break off at the last moment in hopes of bluffing them into leaving. CIOs must master going to manipulative extremes to strengthen the Wolf in the center. The Dove and the Snake best exemplify the extreme binary manipulation behaviors which are most useful to CIOs.

Dove extremes provide fairness and structure to those who want it

CIOs with Dove behaviors are driven by a strong sense of values and beliefs. They have a set of principles around right and wrong which guides all of their actions. They believe that it is important to win the hearts and minds of others in order to expect their co-operation with any initiative. They are often selfless in the extreme and motivated to create a work environment that demonstrates and institutionalizes fairness to everyone in the community. They display the following characteristics:

- Can clearly articulate their values and principles of right and wrong
- Others follow them because they find them inspiring and agree with their values
- Impervious to status and hierarchy, they prefer systems with fairness and equality
- May seem unrealistic, uncompromising or out of touch with others

CIOs with Dove qualities are often very selective about where they work and will strongly scrutinize the leadership of an enterprise and its mission before agreeing to work there. Doves are most likely to gain power when the enterprise is emerging from a period of extreme strife in which corporate ethics may have come into question. A dark-side enterprise would avoid hiring CIOs with these qualities as they actually make others feel badly about themselves. The dark-side executives may worry about a CIO with a strong sense of fairness thinking, *They will take my IT resources and give them to others, and they just won't understand how things really work around here. No, we can't have that because I just figured out how to manipulate the system we have now and it is working fine for me.*

Snake extremes provide adaptability and subterfuge to those who need it

CIOs with Snake behaviors are driven by pragmatism and are willing to be highly adaptable to achieve the greater good. They have a strong sense of goals and objectives, but will make calculated ethical trade-offs to achieve them. They carefully study situations to determine if the methods for achieving their goals require adaptation, or if the goal itself needs changing. They are highly observant, and look for patterns of behaviors in others so that they can predict their movements and find the optimal time to strike. They are highly secretive and willing to use subterfuge, only revealing information or their true motives for doing something if it advances the agenda. They display these characteristics:

- Makes decisions based on the individual situation rather than a rigid set of rules

- Others follow them because they get things done, although it is unclear to observers exactly how they are doing it

- Uses empathy, observation and patience to strategize the best approach way of getting others to cooperate

- May seem untrustworthy to others since their beliefs may appear malleable

- These CIOs excel in dark-side organizations that are immature, highly complex or dysfunctional, and lack clear processes and procedures. They can effectively maneuver in situations where there is a lack of structure and still get things done.

Snake CIOs do less well in light-side enterprises, where their extreme adaptability may make their actions appear contradictory or enigmatic, and therefore render them untrustworthy to others. While staff may enjoy working with these CIOs due to their high degree of empathy, they may find it difficult to follow their lead or replicate their successes since their actions will often be complex, unclear or unsystematic. As a result, Snake CIOs are often less-than-ideal mentors.

The Wolf strives to use manipulation altruistically, rather than for personal gain

CIOs with Wolf qualities will go to both ends of the manipulation spectrum, blending both Dove and Snake tactics at the same time to get the job done. They display a strong sense of values, but are not so inflexible in adhering to them that they cannot get the job done. They strive to be honest and trustworthy, but refuse to be an easy target for other manipulators. Overall, they focus first and foremost on what is best for the enterprise, rather than using their powers of manipulation for personal gain. The line between the two is seldom clear, but that is what the Wolf will strive for each day. In the next few sections we'll explore the specific situations when a CIO is most likely to need to manipulate and the tactics that are most effective for success.

Wolf Packet

There is as much risk in manipulating as there is in telling the truth. CIOs must "pick their poison" and determine which approach is best for them both professionally and ethically. Doves fly high above the earth, but it is an awfully long way to fall. Snakes are firmly on the ground, but must determine how much mud they are willing to slither through to accomplish the goals.

Remember:

- Honesty is not the best policy in every situation
- Manipulation is the dark side of influence
- CIOs must overcome practices that make them more likely to be manipulated
- Dove extremes provide fairness and structure to those who want it
- Snake extremes provide adaptability and subterfuge to those who need it
- The Wolf strives to use manipulation altruistically, rather than for personal gain

10: Treat Colleagues as Friends, but Assume They Are Enemies

The worst that a prince may expect of a people who are unfriendly to him is that they will desert him;

But the hostile nobles he has to fear, not only lest they abandon him, but also because they will turn against him.

For they, being more farsighted and astute, always save themselves in advance, and seek to secure the favor of him whom they hope may be successful.

Machiavelli, *The Prince*

The more they have to lose, the higher the likelihood they will turn on you

How a CIO deals with a new stakeholder is often a key indicator of his manipulation approach. Should a CIO trust all new stakeholders until they give her reason not to, or should she dare to take a wait-and-see approach to ensure she is dealing with a friend rather than a potential enemy? Machiavelli warned that trusting new people below you in the hierarchy usually poses a minimal risk. Unless they are aligned with someone above you, the worst they can do is leave, and there is usually someone to replace them. Executive colleagues are much more dangerous since they have a great deal to lose and are likely to turn and attack someone else to save themselves.

Consider Lori's situation. She has been a CIO in the banking industry for over 20 years and has seen many colleagues come and go. Recently, a new CFO requested a replacement ERP system. Lori implemented the existing system for the previous CFO only two years prior, and while it is not perfect, she believed it was sufficient for the task and that she could modify it to address the new CFO's needs and save the replacement cost. The new CFO, however, was adamant about having the same system he used at his prior company.

Lori has a Dove leadership style, so she gave the new CFO the benefit of the doubt that there really was something different about this new financial system. She assumed the CFO knew what he wanted and really needed this system. She told the CFO that he would struggle to complete the other work he had planned for the next 12 months, but the CFO asked her to trust that he would stand up for him with the other stakeholders. Lori made the mistake of deciding to trust him — classic Dove behavior. When she ran behind schedule and the total IT budget ran significantly over forecast, the CFO skewered her to the Board of Directors. Having trusted the CFO over her own judgment, she had no defense and her reputation was irreparably damaged.

Snakes take nothing for granted and do their research

Paul, a CIO for a pension fund is in a similar circumstance with a new business-unit president. The new president has requested a specific software package with a specific vendor. The request is presented almost as a fait accompli, and Paul is surprised by how far down the path the president has gone without engaging him. Paul does a thorough Internet search on the business-unit president. News articles mention his frequent movements from job to job. There are also tweets about his new colleague and comments on websites that track various corporations. The Internet traffic is mixed about both his management style and his abilities. Some people think he is brilliant, others believe the opposite. He has had two jobs in the past three years and seems to have left each position under somewhat-dubious circumstances.

Paul knows that content on the Internet is rarely accurate, but is bothered by the extreme representations of his new colleague. He decides to proceed cautiously and stall the new president's request by exploring other options and gathering more information directly from him. He does not conclude that his new colleague is either a good or a bad guy, but decides to take the time to find out before investing too much. Given his track record, Paul knows there is a good chance he might leave before any significant implementation decisions are made.

A CIO's eye for detail and analysis skills can be his most useful manipulation tool. While trusting too easily is dangerous, so is rushing to judgment. That's why gathering the appropriate information is critical. When CIOs take the time to do their research and apply their ability to analyze information to situations such as these, they can prevent IT-related disasters from happening due to untrustworthy or misguided stakeholders.

To find the hidden agenda, go to the source

In the previous example, the CIO went to the Internet and other secondary sources to gather information about a new colleague to determine if he was trustworthy. One of the most underutilized sources of useful manipulation information are the colleagues themselves. Consider this common exchange I have with CIOs. The CIO will share, *I don't know if I should trust this guy. He asked for a new software package I don't think he needs, and I don't know why he really wants it or what he is hoping to accomplish. I get the sense there is another agenda here, but I don't know what it is.* Did you ask him? *No.* Why not? *I don't know.*

We often get the impression that a stakeholder has a hidden agenda when we have not actually asked them about it. Technically, their agenda isn't hidden if you haven't asked them for it. CIOs will sometimes fail to ask, either assuming that the colleague should tell them and preferably document it, or they may believe asking them for it directly could be considered impolite. Respectfully questioning a colleague can yield significant information about their trustworthiness. Consider, *I'd like to help. Is there a business issue you are hoping this will fix? I may have some better alternatives for you. Are you open to them? I'm not sure I understand; would you please tell me more?*

The responses may pleasantly surprise the CIO who discovers that her concerns were unwarranted. Or, the colleague's evasion of the questions or inconsistent answers may confirm her suspicions that they walk on the dark side. In either case, the CIO has more information now than she had before. She can determine if she is indeed being manipulated, or will have learned how to better manipulate her colleague.

The Wolf hopes for the best but plans for the worst

Stephen guards his time carefully and doesn't jump when a new stakeholder enters the scene. As CIO for a biotech firm, he works with many entrepreneurial stakeholders who have lots of great ideas. However, as is the case in many innovative environments, there are ideas, and then there are attention spans. Many of his stakeholders are enamored with new ideas but then quickly move on to the next shiny object when it catches their attention. He has been burned multiple times when an excited stakeholder absolutely and desperately needed something, and then disappeared when he lost interest.

As a result, Stephen has adopted a blended grey Wolf-like style of working with new stakeholders, best described as *pragmatic optimism*. The light side of him never doubts their sincerity in proposing new IT-related initiatives, or their sincerity in saying they will dedicate the time required to them. However, the dark side of him always doubts the reality and therefore continuously tests for their commitment without telling them what he is doing. When they approach him with ideas, he engages in their enthusiasm, but makes certain to have them fill out a few light proposal forms. If this task is too much, he knows they are not committed. If they pass that hurdle, then he requests more of their time. If they pass that test, then he continues. If they continue to pass each hurdle he places in front of them, then he knows they are likely worthy of trust.

Wolf Packet

CIOs must use their skills in gathering data and their analytical abilities to assess each new stakeholder individually to determine if they are worthy of trust and an investment of resources. Unfortunately, trust is not one size fits all. Many individuals view trust as a gift and attempt to be worthy of it, but others perceive trusting easily as a sign of weakness. While Doves may argue that doubt is a self-fulfilling prophesy, in reality, Snakes know that trust must be earned rather than given freely for it to have any worth.

Remember:

- The more that your colleagues have to lose, the higher the likelihood they will turn on you
- Snakes take nothing for granted and do their research
- To find the hidden agenda, go to the source
- The Wolf hopes for the best, but plans for the worst

11: Treat Information as a Weapon, and Don't Load the Gun Aimed at You

Before all else, be armed.

Machiavelli, *The Prince*

If their first shot missed, don't offer your enemy a bigger gun

Richard, a CIO in a Western European insurance firm, cannot understand why he is constantly under attack. His colleagues continuously question the cost and value of IT and claim not to understand what IT is doing, even though Richard seems to be communicating with them constantly about costs, budgets, work plans and a wide variety of details. Richard is very open to criticism, has two degrees in engineering and computer sciences and almost 20 years of experience. He knows what he is doing, and believes that overall he is doing a good job. But he feels as though his colleagues are micromanaging and continuously criticizing him with no end in sight.

Traditional IT management guidance advocates that the CIO exercise transparency as a good best practice. Machiavelli believed that first and foremost, a leader must be armed. As we discussed earlier, information is a powerful weapon that a CIO can use to protect himself against the untrustworthy. But a weapon can be turned against those who wield it. CIOs with Dove styles often load the gun of information, and then they are shocked when their colleagues shoot them with it. What do they do next? They gather more information, load the machine gun and hand it over to the hostile colleagues, thinking more information will solve the problem. Do not load the gun.

Richard, the insurance company CIO, is a Dove. He engages in transparency in the extreme. Each time a colleague questions a project or why he is falling behind on a timeline, he shares as much information as he can. When that does not appease them he provides more information, and the frustrating cycle repeats itself. Executives tend to believe that others share information with them so that they can do something with it, even when they are told it is for informational purposes only. The more information a CIO brings forward, the more likely they are to become micromanaged as a result. So CIOs must avoid oversharing at all costs. Fortunately, there are alternatives.

A Snake knows how to hide information in plain sight

Emily, a CIO for a financial services company, is aware of her colleagues' tendencies toward micromanagement. Many members of the executive team are former accountants or financial managers who continuously request large amounts of data to satisfy their analytical tendencies. Unfortunately for Emily, they are like many other executives in that they believe they have the right to act on or make a decision on any information they receive, even if action is not requested.

Fortunately, Emily uses a Snake strategy to cope. She collects, generates and shares massive piles of data with her executives, and intentionally buries key information in places where they are unlikely to find it. Technically, she is being transparent and providing what they requested. In reality, she is avoiding being micromanaged on what really matters. It is a risky strategy — both in the obfuscation and in the perception it may create about Emily. Taken to the extreme, if her colleagues never find anything meaningful in the piles of data, they may decide she is incompetent and stop trusting her on any level.

Sharing too much data conveys a lack of confidence and credibility

CIOs often have a very different concept of transparency than other executives. To CIOs, transparency often means sharing tremendous detail and volumes of data that other executives would never think to share. CIOs must compare the amount of data they share about their operations to how much other executives share, and adjust accordingly. This is particularly critical from a perceptual perspective. If a CIO shares a great deal of information and her peers share little, this sends a signal that they are not peers. One is a service provider who has no choice but to reveal all, and the other is not. Peers and partners share approximately the same amount of information with each other, and CIOs must strive for this ratio as part of the relationship.

CIOs must also be aware that how they share determines whether or not they are trusted. The difference between credibility and trust is that when we trust someone, we stop asking them for data. When CIOs overshare, it is the same as saying, *Don't trust me, I don't know what I'm talking about and I need to prove it to you.* Consider how much data your colleagues are really asking for, and how much of your sharing may be a self-inflicted wound that springs from good intentions. At the same time, trust is a journey of delicate extremes. If we go to the extreme of not sharing enough information initially, we lose the opportunity to gain trust at all. So CIOs should share enough data to gain trust but no more; then share less.

The Wolf shares what is required, but not a data point more

Nick grew up in IT and in the retail industry. As a Wolf CIO he is very judicious about the information he shares with other executives. When an executive asks for status on an IT-related project, he often asks what type of information would be useful for them to have, or how they plan to use the information. By asking clarifying questions, he can target the most appropriate information and is more likely to hit the mark. If he suspects a stakeholder is hostile, he sends less information than requested or delays sending it at all until he is certain of how it will be used. In the past, he would share too much and hope that something in the stack of information was what they needed or wanted.

He has learned to mimic the style of his colleagues in tasks such as requesting funding. For example, he used to do extensive business cases that fit IT industry standards for best practices. He was shocked by how superficial the business cases his colleagues presented to the CEO to request funding were. Then, Nick says, "I realized that the CEO was constantly approving funding for those superficial business cases. And I had to ask why I was putting myself through all this work when it clearly wasn't necessary?" In fact, Nick also realized that by providing excessive information, he actually looked less certain than his colleagues about his business cases and more defensive to his CEO. By applying the grey Wolf tactic of equivalent sharing, that is, sharing as much information as others share with you, CIOs can equalize peer relationships and avoid oversharing.

Wolf Packet

Remember:

- If their first shot missed, don't offer your enemies a bigger gun

- Doves engage in transparency in the extreme and inadvertently invite micromanagement

- A Snake knows how to hide information in plain sight

- Sharing too much data conveys a lack of confidence and credibility

- CIOs should share enough data to gain trust but no more; then share less

- The Wolf shares what is required, but not a data point more

12: Recognize That the Hero Is Often the Arsonist, So Don't Feed the Fire

Men are so controlled by immediate necessities that a Prince who deceives will always find those who let themselves be deceived.

Machiavelli, *The Prince*

Don't turn on the hydrant when you've arrived at a false alarm

What is a CIO to do? *They need it now. They need it right now. Actually, they really needed it yesterday. They have no time to plan ahead, because they are so busy. They never needed it before, but they absolutely need it now. They just thought of it, and it is incredibly important, so important that they don't have time to explain it, or understand what it really does. And everyone else has it, we're pretty sure, so it is urgent that they have it now.* Sound familiar? Many CIOs find themselves faced with urgent requests. Urgency is a little-understood but powerful tool of emotional blackmail. How CIOs deal with it can determine if the CIO is a manipulation master or target.

Machiavelli warned that deceit is easier than one would think, since few of us think beyond the moment at hand. CIOs and IT leaders often have personalities geared toward taking action. This is an excellent trait but it can also make them subject to manipulation. The inclination to take action can often override the instinct to stop and check if we are dealing with a false alarm.

CIOs also consider themselves very logical, and some believe they are more logical than their colleagues in other departments. While this may or may not be true, confidence in one's logic and objectivity can put us into denial about the power our emotions have over us. Urgent requests are often conveyed with powerful emotions, and they elicit powerful emotions. If we are not aware of the dynamic this creates, we can easily lose control of them and become subject to manipulation. When a CIO understands the power of emotion, he can use it in his favor.

Doves rush into the burning house and try to rescue the goldfish

Consider Samuel, a CIO for a defense agency. It seems that virtually every request that comes into IT is urgent or critical in some way. Samuel suspects that while his colleagues do have legitimate critical needs, many of the requests are not really urgent, and his colleagues could have planned ahead if they had wanted to do so. However, each time they come to him with a challenge, they are so agitated and insistent that it is difficult to stop and deal with it as anything but urgent.

Samuel is a Dove in an enterprise full of accidental Snakes. In organizations such as military entities, groups of first responders and industries where many issues are legitimately "life and death," an emotional quality can infiltrate virtually every aspect of decision making. On some level the very good, light-side players actually come to believe that virtually every decision they make, from weaponry to email, has a life-and-death implication to it. In such emotionally charged environments, they often accidentally slip over to the dark side by not questioning their assumptions, and manipulation becomes rife.

If, for example, Samuel were to push back and say that an urgent request was not indeed critical on some level, a colleague could imply that his failure to cooperate was endangering lives. While they may not entirely believe this to be true, the emotional intensity of the environment can block objective decision making, and the players may blackmail each other continuously and over the smallest issues without realizing it.

Sometimes you are your own Snake in hero's clothing

It is important to note, however, that CIOs and IT executives often happily play into the manipulation and become their own Snake. Many CIOs either secretly or overtly enjoy the opportunity to respond to the urgent request, strap on their "hero capes" and save the day. They get an emotional rush and satisfaction in working under pressure and doing the seemingly impossible. The rush is addictive, so when the urgent requests come, they don't even attempt to filter then out, and they seek out the rush like an addict. They become complicit in their own blackmail. This dynamic is best exemplified by the reality that sometimes the arsonist is the firefighter. If no one is setting a fire, some firefighters have been known to set one themselves so that they can feel like heroes.

Stakeholders soon learn that CIOs and IT enjoy the fire of urgency, so they continuously feed it to them. They learn that as long as they tag something as urgent, they never have to fill out a form or plan ahead, and the cycle continues. Everyone gets something out of the arrangement.

One of the things that can interrupt the cycle of emotional blackmail is betrayal. Manipulative stakeholders will often fan the flames of urgency, and enlist the CIO by calling him an ally, a friend and a compatriot. Then, when the urgent request is fulfilled, the CIO is suddenly a stranger again and relegated to service provider status. The CIO, who expected a closer relationship from the bargain, feels betrayed by the stakeholder.

Even worse, if the urgent request is fulfilled poorly in the eyes of the stakeholder, then often to the shock of the CIO, the "ally" will turn against him and place the blame of failure squarely on IT. When urgent requests fail to result in durable friendships, or a colleague turns on him, these are indicators that the CIO was actually being manipulated by the colleague from the beginning, even if the colleague did not intend it. And in other cases, the colleague's manipulation was clearly intentional.

Wolves break the cycle to create healthier behaviors and outcomes

Unfortunately, when the cycle of emotional blackmail is broken by betrayal, resentment and irreparable damage can occur. CIOs can take constructive measures to break the cycle and build new patterns of behavior that will benefit everyone involved. To prevent the cycle, CIOs should document and track urgent requests so that they can analyze the pattern of urgency. As one Wolf CIO noted, "It turns out that all of the urgent requests were coming from one or two stakeholders, and they were minor players in the organization who were being ignored by others and wanted attention." These stakeholders tend to notice that CIOs and IT leaders, being very process-oriented and egalitarian, often treat all stakeholders the same way. Although this democratic ethic is admirable, CIOs must take care to manage the time they spend with each colleague.

CIOs should vary their approach on a situational basis. If a colleague rarely asks for an urgent request and the CIO has little reason to distrust them, they may take the calculated risk of proceeding with the request. Alternately, they may test each urgent request in a minor way. For example, one CIO noted that he would require anyone with an urgent request to get a signature from their manager confirming that the request was urgent and verifying the anticipated benefits of the work. This small requirement managed to deter the vast majority of urgent requests with minimal fuss or collateral damage.

Other CIOs break the cycle of urgency by respectfully insisting on the answers to simple questions such as, *Why do you need it now? How much revenue do we lose per week if you don't get it? Do we get a fine for not having this? If so, how much and what is the likelihood we will get the fine? Who is harmed if you don't get it now? Who benefits if we wait and do it differently? Are you willing to pay the premium for rushing this? Do the additional benefits cover the cost of the rush premium?* By engaging colleagues in this level of discussion, it can break the emotional cycle and get stakeholders to think more objectively about their requests. The tactic does require the strength of a Wolf, however, since the CIO must not back down in the face of pressure and must insist that her colleagues actually stop and answer the questions.

Give them what they really want, rather than what they asked for

When dealing with truly powerful stakeholders who appear to be acting deceitfully, CIOs must manage a delicate balance. Consider Lauren, a Wolf CIO for a private equity firm, who was faced with an urgent request from the CEO. He wanted a new customer relationship management system implemented immediately. He informed Lauren that another CEO he knew had implemented the system in six months, and he wanted it done in three. While the CEO claimed business reasons for the investment, Lauren knew he had a very competitive personal relationship with the other CEO. She suspected even her CEO did not realize the real reasons he wanted the system.

In a Snake-like manner, she asked if she could contact the CIO of the other CEO, *to gather information to help accelerate the implementation*, and was told yes. Soon thereafter, she reported back to her CEO that the implementation of the impressive system had cost the other company $18 million. She told him that she would be happy to implement this in their company as well, so long as the CEO understood that the cost would be double given that they were dealing with half the timeline. The CEO dropped his request for the system, *since he no longer needed it*.

Having won the battle, and to ensure she also won the war, Lauren worked to quickly find her CEO a less expensive, innovative investment to implement that he could show off to the other CEO. In this Dove-like manner, she would eventually be able to provide him with what he really wanted, as opposed to what he had actually asked for from her. Despite the danger of the cycle of emotional blackmail, everyone deserves to have at least some of their emotional needs met to avoid an unfortunate binary extreme. Lauren recognized the significance of the CEO's backing down from an extreme emotional request. But her empathy for him led her to her blended grey Wolf approach of take and give, and helped ensure a happy CEO and healthier environment for everyone.

Wolf Packet

Sometimes others deceive us, and other times we deceive ourselves. Successfully navigating deceit entails getting beyond what we or someone else needs, and understanding what we truly want and what motivates us. The most difficult lies to discern are those we tell ourselves and others from good intentions and from force of habit. Regularly ask yourself the question, *What am I lying to myself about and how am I part of the cycle?*

Remember:

- Don't turn on the hydrant when you've arrived at a false alarm
- Doves rush into the burning house and try to rescue the goldfish
- Sometimes you are your own Snake in hero's clothing
- Wolves break the cycle to create healthier behaviors and outcomes
- Give them what they really want, rather than what they asked for

13: Ruthlessly Keep Others From Wasting IT's Time

The experience of our own times has shown that those princes have achieved great things who made small account of good faith, and who understood by cunning to circumvent the intelligence of others;

And that in the end they got the better of those whose actions were dictated by loyalty and good faith.

Machiavelli, *The Prince*

If you do not treat your time as valuable, no one else will

CIOs strive to be partners with their business colleagues. True partnerships are not what many of us think they are. A partnership is a reciprocal relationship between parties of approximately equal power and status. This is where IT relationships with the rest of the enterprise often fall short. When in an order-taker relationship, IT may feel that it is giving while the rest of the enterprise is taking. This kind of relationship often evolves because IT believes it is in a weaker position due to previous delivery challenges, or that this is simply its appropriate role.

Status is often a result of power. The ability to make things happen raises the real or perceived status of an individual or group relative to others. Status is also a result of stance — the signals individuals or groups send out regarding how they perceive themselves, and how others should perceive them. CIOs often accidentally send out signals of lower status. Machiavelli advised that it is appropriate for a leader to break promises when others break theirs. Yet CIOs rarely do this and end up sending a signal that they are not free to break their promises and thus are lower status than their colleagues.

The Dove approach lowers your status and damages partnerships

Consider Gavin, who works for a local hospital. He knows he has some colleagues he can count on as business sponsors and uses them whenever he is able. When his sponsors take the time to engage, the projects tend to go smoothly and everyone is happy with the outcomes. He is aware, however, that specific stakeholders have a track record of not engaging. When those colleagues request IT, he completed the project but compensates for the stakeholders by assigning stronger project leads and larger teams so that they can take on the role the project sponsor normally would.

While one can argue that this is highly pragmatic and ultimately fulfills the business needs, this approach has significant collateral damage associated with it. His colleagues have learned, *The less I do, the more*

IT does. So why do more? And they learn to rationalize their behavior by saying, *My time is more valuable than theirs, so I shouldn't waste my time on IT projects anyway.* By trying to avoid the problem, he has inadvertently fed the problem and damaged IT's status in the organization. Colleagues who initially engaged and behaved as good partners felt like they were being penalized for their good behavior and started disengaging. Everyone ultimately lost as they manipulated each other into failure.

Snakes provide prompt service from the worst project team they have

Megan works in the pharmaceutical industry, where stakeholders can be demanding and the sheer volume of IT-related requests can be difficult to manage. When project sponsors disengage, it makes her job even more difficult. Many of her colleagues are outstanding project sponsors who engage well and help make her job a joy. Certain other colleagues continuously demand IT on a tight schedule, then disappear and seemingly expect it to appear magically with no time investment on their part.

Megan has adopted a Snake strategy best referred to as negative reinforcement. While a Dove would compensate for a poor project sponsor by applying strong resources, a Snake penalizes the sponsor by assigning the weakest project team they have available. Megan takes her youngest and least-skilled project team and pairs them with the poor project sponsor.

When the poor project sponsor complains, she feigns innocence, *Well, they are new but everyone has to start somewhere, don't they? If you could coach them through the process I would greatly appreciate it. I'm sure you're not asking for special treatment in requesting a new team as that wouldn't be fair, would it? No, I know that's not what you meant. I'm sure you'll love working with our rookies.* While this high-risk behavior may endanger the project in the short term, over the long term it will create more regard for IT's time and will teach dark-side players to behave better.

A Wolf demands reciprocity and holds everyone accountable

Most IT shops are good at estimating IT's and a vendor's time and materials before beginning a project. Only a small percentage does the same with their colleagues. This sets up an uneven and unrealistic dynamic in the organization where we convince ourselves that the time of our colleagues is optional for the successful completion of the initiatives. In many ways we are not being clear or upfront with our colleagues about what their role really is in success. We may assume they should know what their role is, but they rarely do, and will almost never take the time to find out.

Whenever Raja, a business-unit CIO for a large telecommunications company, launches a project, he estimates the time and materials required from the sponsor and key stakeholders in the same way he would for an external consultant. Then, he sets up milestones for both the time and the materials, including key information deliverables, and holds the sponsor to the milestones. If the sponsor falls significantly behind in their commitment, he stops the project.

As Raja explains, "If they disappear from the project, it is like saying it is no longer important to them. If it is not important enough that they spend time on it, then why is it important that I and my team spend time on it?" Our Wolf CIO Raja believes it is crucial to be as clear as possible about what sponsors need to do at the outset, and then hold them accountable. Otherwise, sponsors will come to believe that IT is not actually being honest when they say that they need them involved in the project.

Some CIOs avoid stopping projects because they worry about creating a wave of constant conflict. While this is potentially true, in reality, it can take as few as one project pause or cancellation to demonstrate to the enterprise that the CIO is serious about needing sponsor engagement in IT-related projects. CIOs should consider that one visible, difficult confrontation can send a message and change the behavior of current and potential sponsors in the long run.

Wolf Packet

When CIOs allow stakeholders to disappear and break their commitment to projects and IT-related initiatives, it often sends the wrong message. Sponsors come to believe that their time is valuable, and IT's time is not. They will believe that their status is high, and IT's is low. CIOs often avoid forcing engagement because they are overly focused on being on time and on budget. Sponsors notice this, and can use it against CIOs.

Remember:

- If you do not treat your time as valuable, no one else will
- The Dove approach in a dark-side enterprise lowers your status and damages partnerships
- Snakes provide prompt service to poor partners from the worst project team they have
- A Wolf demands reciprocity and holds everyone accountable

14: Combine the Wolf's Power With Manipulation Tactics to Maximize Impact

The Romans in the early beginning of their power already employed fraud,

Which it has ever been necessary for those to practice who from small beginnings wish to rise to the highest degree of power;

And then it is the less censurable the more it is concealed, as was that practiced by the Romans.

Machiavelli, *The Discourses*

Use power to create an impact and manipulation as the targeting system

Both power and manipulation are important leadership tools when used separately. As Machiavelli noted, they are particularly effective when used in combination. Sometimes, manipulation alone is not enough to achieve our goals. Power when used alone can be dangerous because it creates collateral damage, the scale and impact of which is often unpredictable.

Traditional management advice instructs us to minimize collateral damage. Machiavelli would disagree with this assessment. This may be the appropriate approach in light-side enterprises; however, when dealing with a dark-side culture, force is often necessary. However, even when dealing with the dark side, a Wolf CIO must avoid being reckless with power to ensure that the collateral damage is neither excessive nor aimed in the wrong direction, such as at oneself. Power and manipulation are thus most effective when used together skillfully.

A large dose of manipulation can serve as a Wolf CIO's targeting system, enabling him to use a smaller amount of power to maximum effect. In essence in this combination, a CIO can minimize both the use of force and the damage, but achieve maximum effect — essentially a precision strike. Consider the alternative — use a large amount of power with minimum targeting where we hope to hit our target by attacking and leveling the general area around it — an area bombardment.

Apply precision strikes to prevent smaller problems from becoming larger ones

The collateral damage in area bombardments may exceed the value of the target. Many enterprises use the bombardment strategy. For example, creating a policy that *no one may work from home anymore* because several staff may have abused the practice, rather than focusing on disciplining the abusers and using them as a warning to others as a precision strike. The bombardment policy can demoralize staff who will feel penalized for the behavior of others, and they often lose faith in their enterprise leadership. Such collateral damage can be avoided.

Precision strikes are useful particularly in situations where a Wolf CIO wants to take preventative measures to ensure that smaller problems do not become much larger ones, such as total warfare. As we have discussed, CIOs are often in hostile situations not of their choosing. These situations require them to go on the offensive and deal with situations that can become larger and more dangerous if not dealt with quickly. By applying manipulation techniques with a dose of power before a larger part of the enterprise is affected, CIOs can delay or prevent all-out warfare situations, where the collateral damage is likely to be much higher.

Break up a mass revolt early by targeting the middle of the herd

How can a CIO stop passive aggression of a project team from growing into a mass revolt? Unfortunately, CIOs must periodically deal with teams that are working slowly, minimally, or behaving passively and refusing to get work done. When the team has bad intentions, a lot of manipulation with a little bit of power is the CIO's best Machiavellian solution to deal with the situation. In cases where a group bands together to "rebel," they often believe that there is safety in the herd and that the leader will be unwilling or unable to punish so many of them. An effective Wolf CIO will ensure that the individuals cannot either hide or find protection in the herd, and in fact find ways to use the herd mentality against them.

William, a CIO from a food services company, described his tactic for dealing with the situation, best described as *firing into the middle of the herd*. "I identified someone on the project team who was an ok performer and who the team really liked. Then I waited. When he said something in a project team meeting that sounded a little bit like he was objecting, I yelled, screamed, and threw him out of the room and off the project team in front of everyone."

William went on to explain "The team was completely shaken both by the scene, and because they knew he was not the worst performer in the room. As a result, they felt that none of them were safe any longer. After that, the project team finally started moving. If I had chosen the weakest performer or someone everyone disliked, then rest of the team would have still felt they were safe in the herd and the tactic would not have worked." Such tactics, while seemingly unfair to some, prevent larger-scale damage such as the failure of the project itself, or the elimination of the entire project team due to nonperformance in the extreme.

Use a precision strike to prevent collateral damage from coming back at you

Roger, a CIO from a North American semiconductor company, had suffered a security breach resulting in a significant loss of intellectual property. The CEO asked Roger to find the source of the breach. The source turned out to be another senior executive whose laptop was compromised when he used it to access "inappropriate" websites. This particular executive and Roger had never gotten along. As Roger described the situation, "He would disagree with me at every opportunity. Whether in front of the CEO, the board of directors or any business-unit president, he was always arguing with any point that I made, and I had no idea why."

The situation, however, created a significant shift in their relationship. As Roger continued, "Now we're the best of friends and we work very well together." How did Roger accomplish this miracle? He discovered that his nemesis was the source of the breach. His nemesis panicked, fearful that the CEO would discover his inappropriate behavior. He asked Roger if he had to tell the CEO what happened. Roger told him, "I have to tell him that you were the source of the breach. I do not have to tell him exactly what you were doing. But from now on, use your home computer for that stuff and don't let me catch you again." His nemesis immediately became his friend.

This high-risk situation happens for CIOs around the world every day given the access they have to information about the Internet activities of their senior colleagues. Upon reporting such inappropriate online behavior, some CIOs have suffered significant collateral damage, as they found themselves objects of distrust from the entire executive team afterward. In extreme cases, CIOs who have reported inappropriate online behaviors were subject to retaliation by CEOs who felt forced into taking action against executive team members they had hired or liked.

While such retaliation is illegal, it is difficult to prevent or prove in a court of law. Sam decided that since his colleague had not broken any laws, and the company was not significantly harmed in the situation, he would omit the details of the inappropriate behavior in his report to the CEO, and keep his colleague from possibly being fired. He avoided all the potential collateral damage from falling back on him, and received an improved relationship with his colleague.

Avoiding management by bombardment to prevent future unrest

How should CIOs deal with situations that are certain to make them lose allies and support? Consider the common situation where a CIO's enterprise goes into cost-cutting mode. Perhaps the economy has deeply impacted your industry suddenly, or a new competitor has taken some of your business, so the enterprise is cutting costs until they find a good way of dealing with the competitor. CIOs in these situations are often asked to cut the budget deeply, frequently starting with the project list and capital budget.

Imagine a CIO who has been asked to cut the IT budget by 20%. The most traditional management tactic is to cut the project budget of each stakeholder equally, by 20% In a light-side environment, stakeholders are likely to view this approach as fair, and feel positively about the CIO and negatively about the situation. However, in dark-side enterprises, this tactic does not have the same effect. Stakeholders will perceive that the CIO has essentially executed an area bombardment on all his stakeholders.

They will complain, *This is not fair, we really needed that IT project and we haven't had any new IT in forever. The other business units always get what they want and this won't make a dent in their ability to execute, but once again it will affect us.* The other stakeholders will say, *We're the most strategic part of the business and we bring in all the revenue, so it makes no sense to cut our IT; that CIO doesn't understand this business at all.* In a dark-side culture, by cutting all of his colleague's IT projects equally, the

CIO simply ensures that all of his colleagues now dislike him equally.

What the Wolf CIO would do is precisely focus the entire project budget remaining on the colleagues he most needs to win over, or who are the most critical to enterprise success. Those colleagues are now the CIO's friends. Everyone else is now an enemy, but at least now the CIO knows who is an enemy, and who is a friend. The collateral damage has been focused in a specific area, rather than becoming a generalized attack on the whole of the enterprise, risking the CIO's reputation and position.

Your paws will never be entirely clean, so expect the paw prints to lead back to you

It is important for manipulation novices to experiment with these tactics carefully when learning how to use them and testing their own ethical boundaries. Practice does make perfect but be aware that the more tactics you practice, the more likely others will notice. The more colleagues who know about your deceits, the more likely someone will tell and you will be found out. The more subterfuge you use, the more likely it is you will lose track of your lies and trap yourself. So proceed with caution. Even the most stealthy and manipulative Wolf will be caught sooner or later. It may be bad luck or perhaps nature's way of keeping us in check. In either case, consider your options.

One option is to move to the extreme Dove side and tell the truth. While this may convince others that your intentions were good, and that you were behaving in this manner for the greater good, you will have now confirmed that you are a manipulator and are therefore untrustworthy. In a light-side enterprise they may forgive you, but it is unlikely they will ever trust you again. A dark-side organization likely did not trust you in the first place, as they tend not to trust anyone. But now that you have been caught, they will not respect you either, since you were weren't good enough at manipulating to avoid getting caught.

Your second option is to stick with the lie and then lie some more to cover your tracks. You will have now moved deeply into the Snake side. In a light-side organization they are unlikely to suspect what you are doing. As long as they cannot prove you lied, they will likely give you the benefit of the doubt, since they will find it hard to believe that anyone could lie that much. In a dark-side organization, they are more likely to suspect what you are doing, but if they cannot prove it, they will simply be sure to watch you more carefully in the future. Some may also admire what you did and consider you a worthy ally going forward.

Wolf Packet

A Wolf CIO is always prepared and willing to adapt to the situation. Keep in mind that getting caught is not a signal to stop manipulating, but to practice more. By using power and manipulation in the right proportions, you can limit the collateral damage, maximize the effect and minimize the likelihood of getting caught. A skillful balance will earn the admiration of followers who will view the CIO as having empathy, being measured in her actions and merciful to those she did not attack.

Remember:

- Use power to create an impact and manipulation as the targeting system
- Apply precision strikes to prevent smaller problems from becoming larger ones
- Break up a mass revolt early by targeting the middle of the herd
- Use a precision strike to prevent collateral damage from coming back at you
- Avoiding management by bombardment to prevent future unrest
- Your paws will never be entirely clean, so expect the paw prints to lead back to you

Wolf CIOs grow power. They master the art of manipulation. When power and manipulation are used together, they are exponentially more effective. As noted, by combining a large dose of manipulation as the targeting system with a small dose of power, CIOs can focus the effect and create a precision strike to prevent smaller issues from becoming larger ones. But not always. Sometimes, there is nothing we can do to prevent small issues from becoming large issues, and large issues from becoming total warfare.

Sometimes the war comes to our door without our having the opportunity to prevent it. Then we have no choice but to deal with it as best we can. Other times, we go to the battlefield because we know someone has to take on the fight, and a healthy Wolf will feel obligated to do so. In either case, power and manipulation are still the core toolset. But in total warfare, rather than focusing the effect with a precision strike, a Wolf CIO must learn to scale up the impact of power and manipulation across a large number of targets simultaneously, and take control of a large territory. Only then will the Wolf CIO have come to its full strength and potential.

Let's go to war.

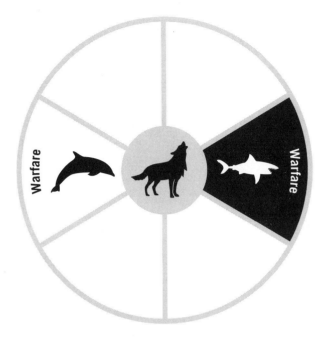

Section III: Warfare

No one should ever submit to an evil for the sake of avoiding a war.

For a war is never avoided, but is only deferred to one's own disadvantage.

Machiavelli, *The Prince*

15: Master Multilateral Wars of Expansion to Grow the Enterprise and IT

War is made on a commonwealth for two reasons: to subjugate it and for fear of being subjugated by it.

Machiavelli, *The Discourses*

Scale up and amplify manipulation and power multilaterally

The difference between power and manipulation and warfare is scale. Warfare requires a leader who can take the elements of power and manipulation, scale them up exponentially and manage multiple levels of warfare simultaneously. There is nothing pretty about warfare, and fortunately, only a handful of CIOs in the Armed Forces fight the lethal wars in real battlefields and protect the rest of us. But it is essential that CIOs learn from them and master the Machiavellian principles of running multilateral campaigns in order to succeed in the complex world of IT today.

As Machiavelli noted, we make war on others because they have something that we want, or because we fear them and decide the best course of action is a preemptive strike. We attack external competitors to create growth opportunities for the enterprise. And as

CIOs, sometimes we are under attack by competitors for the same reason. While being attacked is, at times, a sign of weakness, Machiavelli pointed out that being attacked can also be an indicator that you already have the upper hand.

Warfare is by definition, a team sport. CIOs cannot wage war alone. Success is dependent upon having a strong IT leadership team that works as a unit, a large number of loyal troops and strong allies who are willing to partner with IT, behave strategically and help grow the enterprise. Achieving this level of complexity requires the CIO to deploy multiple tactics on a mass scale, monitor a changing battlefield, recognize opportunities when they are handed to him and be willing to create mass destruction when it is required. Warfare is not for the faint of heart, but as Machiavelli noted, CIOs who avoid taking it on do so at their own peril. If you wait until the enemy troops are at your doorstep, it is already too late.

Unilateral methods of warfare are expedient but inherently unstable

One method of unilateral warfare is the coup, or assassination. In one of our earlier examples, Chris, a CIO, fired Tim for speaking badly to senior executives about him and attempting to usurp his position. Had Tim succeeded, he would have successfully assassinated Chris, staged a coup and been in charge of IT.

Assassinations shift leadership quickly and with minimal bloodshed, and thus might appear an attractive tactic. But in warfare, there is no such thing as a quick fix. Others would have had little reason to be loyal to Tim after his unilateral actions and every reason to fear him. Upon observing the assassination tactic, our colleagues often master it and turn it against their new overlord.

Usurpers tend to succeed in dark-side enterprises that have developed a taste for blood. Unfortunately, they rarely stop at one assassination and often will have multiple CIOs in a short period of time as a result. So while unilateral methods of warfare may appear attractive, the peace is usually short, and ends rather abruptly and definitively. Thus in waging war, CIOs must always be thoughtful about the quality of the peace. Multilateral approaches such as creating alliances, fostering followership, fighting long battles and large-scale manipulation are time-consuming and treacherous. But when the war is won, the peace is more likely to be stable and durable because so many of the populace will be invested in its success and yours.

Extreme Animal Ecosystem: Binary Warfare Animals

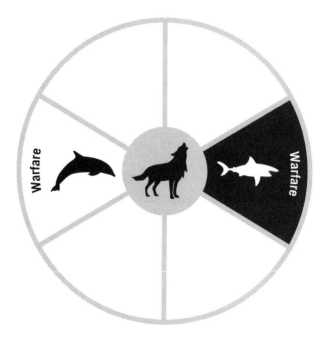

There are light-side approaches in warfare, and then there is the grey Wolf, who embodies the qualities of the Machiavellian general. Wolf CIOs apply a mix of the light and dark tactics even in warfare. They go to the light side to inspire loyalty and make others want to follow them, and to the dark side to create discipline in the troops and fear in the enemy. They are the leaders who make you brave enough to follow them into the unknown, but who you do not dare to cross. In this third and final discipline of warfare, the journey to becoming a grey Wolf begins by learning to go to the extremes of light and dark, best exemplified by the Dolphin and Shark.

Dolphins are highly social and can consume vast schools of information

CIOs with Dolphin characteristics create follower-ship by making people want to go with them by making the experience enjoyable. Dolphins are the extroverts of the animal kingdom; they truly enjoy being with and leading people, and prefer peace to warfare. They consume information like they consume schools of fish. They gather information about their followers, their enemies and their environment, analyze and use it to prevent warfare but succeed at it when they have no choice. Others follow them because they know that wherever they go, the journey will be a fun one and that even when the going gets tough, their Dolphin CIO genuinely cares about them. Partners seek them out because they want them on their team, and seek to be part of theirs.

They exhibit the following characteristics:

- Extroverted with excellent people skills; they prefer peace but amass and use information as a weapon
- They create a positive team environment to attract followers and partners
- Demonstrate genuine caring and empathy toward IT staff and colleagues

- Make the work fun and enjoyable, but can become lost in the myriad relationships and information they gather, and fail to prioritize among them

- May not be taken seriously by others, especially by enemy forces

Extreme Dolphin CIOs do well in highly collaborative environments and peaceful cultures where the enterprise goals and values are clear and favor the people of the enterprise, rather than in enterprises where profitability or the shareholders come first. They tend to take significant time to socialize change, and gather tremendous input from many stakeholders. When the pace of change accelerates, often their social and analytical tactics cannot keep up. If the industry's competitive environment becomes extreme, these CIOs may be seen as too "nice" to take the enterprise into battle with a more aggressive competitor.

Sharks kill with extreme prejudice and leave few survivors

CIOs with Shark characteristics are aggressive in the extreme. Others follow them because they know that in a battle these CIOs will win, and they fear being on the losing side. They amass a wide arsenal of powerful weapons, and create a fearsome reputation by taking down any competitors who get in their way. They do form alliances, but due to their fearsome nature, usually their alliances are only with other Sharks. This makes them quite powerful, but if Shark partners sense weakness or blood in the water, the partnership will devolve into total annihilation. If a Shark is assassinated, the coup will also result in a bloodbath because the formerly fearful followers are likely to run wild with the threat of the Shark removed.

Sharks exhibit the following characteristics:

- Excellent fighting skills; they amass large-scale firepower and strong alliances
- Aggressively drive results, often through negative incentives
- Others follow and partner with them for protection as well as for fear of reprisals, and because they believe this team will win
- Will achieve results at almost any price to self or others
- May be viewed as vicious, destructive, noncollaborative or self-focused

CIO Sharks do well in highly competitive, dark-side environments where their colleagues are also Sharks, relentlessly focused on delivering results. In enterprises where the shareholder comes first, or where the market is highly competitive, these CIOs can win and protect their teams. They are vulnerable to all the other Sharks, however, because any mistake may lead the others to sense blood in the water and trigger a feeding frenzy.

Shark CIOs are often also the go-to leaders for light-side enterprises in a crisis or turnaround situation where major, unpopular changes such as layoffs need to happen quickly in order for the enterprise to survive. Extreme Sharks are rarely in any one place for the long haul as a result. In turnaround situations, the level of collateral damage they create is usually so great that Sharks cannot stay and lead in the restructured light-side environment.

Wolves are both Dolphin and Shark in warfare

To succeed in warfare, the CIO must master a blend of the Dolphin's social and information analysis skills and the Shark's fighting skills. By periodically going to the extremes and demonstrating both understanding of their people and the environment and the ability to dispatch threats with extreme prejudice, they can grow and protect their territory while building a lasting peace.

They are highly disciplined and able to create well-organized campaigns that require long-term planning and multilateral tactics. They are also highly adaptable and can analyze large amounts of information, finding the most important data points, and adjust their tactics dynamically to suit the situation. The more Dolphin and Shark skills the Wolf builds, the more successful his campaigns will be, and the less likely it is he will be attacked in the future. The Wolf's abilities enable him to grow a small territory into a larger one, and protect that territory in the long run.

Wolf Packet

Warfare is messy and complex. We would prefer not to engage in it, but we have little choice but to engage with a mission to succeed. The alternatives are much worse. To succeed in warfare, CIOs must be able to process vast amounts of data, analyze multiple variables in motion at the same time, and then modify their power and manipulation tactics as required. Fortunately, CIOs tend to be exceptionally good at handling large amounts of data, and data of significant complexity. When they apply those skills to warfare, success is virtually assured.

Remember:

- Scale up and amplify manipulation and power multilaterally to succeed at warfare
- Unilateral methods of warfare are expedient but inherently unstable
- Dolphins are highly social and can consume vast schools of information
- Sharks kill with extreme prejudice and leave few survivors
- Wolves are neither Dolphin nor Shark in warfare but rather are both at the same time

16: Engage Lieutenants to Scale Up Your Power and Manipulation

The first opinion one forms of a Prince, and of his understanding, is by observing the men he has around him.

Machiavelli, *The Discourses*

Use the IT leadership team to scale up, or rescale them out

No matter how much power or manipulation skill CIOs acquire, their reach and range is always limited if they behave as independent entities and cannot execute to scale. Since we are discussing warfare, execute is meant quite literally. In warfare, one must be able to dispatch multiple enemies or potential enemies at one time. Level one in multilateral warfare and creating scale is developing a high-performing IT leadership team, and ensuring that they march in lockstep toward the strategy. Many CIOs believe that they have good relationships and partner well with the CEO, CFO and other leaders in the enterprise. They feel comfortable collaborating as well as saying no periodically in their peer-to-peer and executive relationships. Unfortunately, when their direct reports engage with IT and business colleagues, the situation may be quite different and might actually undermine the CIO, his strategy and his ability to execute to scale.

As one CIO described it, *No matter how many times I tell my team that they can say 'no' to their colleagues, they are either people pleasers or conflict avoidant so they simply refuse to. They don't mean any harm, but will do almost anything to avoid saying no to them or me. So they will try to keep secret from me things they should not be working on, because they are so anxious to please their colleagues and afraid I will tell them not to work on their colleagues' nonstrategic requests.* The other extreme also happens and can undermine the most Machiavellian CIO: *No matter what I do, I can't get my team to say 'yes' to their colleagues. The team wants to do the right thing, but if their colleagues don't do the right thing the right way, then the answer is 'no' and there is no discussion or negotiation. Sometimes they are doing it because they feel overworked, but in either case I feel undermined.*

As Machiavelli noted, a leader is judged by those with whom she surrounds herself. If an IT leadership team accidentally or intentionally undermines the CIO, or is occupied with infighting and executing each other rather than the strategy, then the CIO is weakened, and will not be able to scale his tactics to succeed in either offensive or defensive wars. So CIOs must select the best lieutenants, and manage them cohesively.

Otherwise they must rescale either their approach or their team. Only then can they begin to scale up their power and manipulation tactics to succeed.

Dolphins must avoid creating teams that are too large to control

Dolphin CIOs who enjoy managing people often commit the error of having as many direct reports as possible. These CIOs may have teams of 10 or more, spend significant time in skip-level meetings and have an "open-door" policy with everyone else. Kevin was one such CIO in the manufacturing industry. He took this approach not only because he liked people, but also because he believed the entire IT department needed a transformation to fix a wide variety of technical and staffing issues.

Unfortunately, 10 months into his role, he had morale issues with his team and credibility issues with his colleagues. The team behaved in a manner Kevin considered "gossipy," and devolved into subgroups that resemble school cliques. When the performance of one team member was weak, they alternately defended one another or assigned blame rather than solving the problem at hand. Kevin liked to positively motivate his team rather than set boundaries, which unfortunately did not work with his now-dark-side team. When he recognized a strong performer, others expressed resentment. The dissension in the team deepened to the point where little got accomplished and colleagues turned to outside providers to get strategic work done.

When a team is so large that it lacks attention and clear direction from the leader, the members will turn to each other in a negative fashion, and the team environment will degrade. Kevin's situation was compounded by his Dolphin-like open-door policy, which ensured he was continuously in meetings with staff and colleagues, and booked, double-booked or triple-booked with an increasing number of issues and complaints from colleagues that could have been solved if he had turned his attention to fixing the team.

Sharks must avoid accidentally scaling up fear and paralyzing followers

Simon is a Shark CIO in the shipping industry who is having difficulty understanding why he cannot accelerate the pace of IT change in his organization. He created a digital strategy working with the other C-level executives, gained budget resources, developed personal credibility and set a compelling agenda to deliver competitive advantage. Unfortunately, he didn't get his IT leadership team and department to move.

He had a deputy, Daniel, to whom all of the key IT managers reported, so that Simon was able to focus on large-scale strategic issues. Daniel oversaw the work, did all the performance reviews and handled all personnel matters. Simon was frustrated that when he dealt with the IT managers directly, they looked to Daniel before agreeing to cooperate with him. If Daniel was not in the room, Simon suspected the team talked with him first before agreeing to do what he asked. The more resistant the managers were to his direction, the more aggressive he became, firing off angry emails, threatening and insisting on more accountability to him. While these aggressive tactics initially worked to get the team to move quickly and be more responsive, the more Simon used the tactic, the worse the results became.

During his frequent "attacks" the entire team would freeze in place as prey would in the face of a predator; then they actively tried to avoid future encounters. Rather than drawing the team toward him, Simon scaled up the fear factor to an unacceptable level and caused them to avoid engaging with him and subsequently, the digital strategy. Simon the Shark became a hostile, disconnected nonentity to them, and the digital strategy came to a standstill. While Shark like aggression is periodically useful in getting a team to move quickly, when used in the extreme it only scales up paralysis, as the entire team becomes too fearful to move.

Wolves demand pack behavior from the pack members

Wolf CIOs create strong, highly coordinated wolf packs, then strategically engage them in their power and manipulation maneuvers to great effect. They create a level of team discipline and subtlety rarely seen outside of the pack. Bruce, a Wolf CIO of a restaurant chain, was selective with his direct reports, rewarding them well but aggressively dealing with those who strayed from the pack. In IT, traditional performance management systems reward individual achievement. IT processes segment work into individual tasks and disincentivize the team behaviors that today's dynamic IT environment requires.

The interview process and metrics Bruce designed for the team targeted both individual and multilevel team metrics. Bruce explains, "Each IT manager must provide evidence of their ability to successfully lead their own teams, and act as members of both the IT team and business partner teams. As such, each individual's reward system is based heavily upon the team's success. It is not possible for an IT manager to get a top rating if he cannot work well with others."

By making collaboration a requirement for his team, Bruce neutralized the potential for infighting and the individualistic behaviors that can degrade into laying blame and conflict. If a team member was a strong individual performer but did not collaborate well with colleagues outside of IT, Bruce made an assessment. He notes, "If the business partner is trying to collaborate and my direct report is not, no matter how well he performs, I will either fire him or demote him to a more tactical role. If the partner is a poor collaborator, then

I work with his manager to correct the situation, and protect my team member." This grey Wolf CIO tactic is best described as *"collaborate or else."* It combines the Dolphin-like desire for teamwork with Shark-like consequences for noncompliance for pack members and those who interact with the pack.

Wolves scale up power through clarity and discipline

In order for a Wolf CIO to lead in a warfare situation, the wolf pack must work closely together as a unit. To ensure this, these CIOs engage in Dolphin-like communications, with Shark-like aggression. As Ralph, a Wolf CIO for a military organization explained, "I made the strategy clear, but I also taught the team to think by consistently asking them the simple questions. Before they made any decision, they had to ask themselves the questions I gave them, including 'Is this direction consistent with the strategy or inconsistent? What are the risks of doing this? What are the risks of not doing this? What are the interdependencies, and who is affected? Is this likely to be a political decision and, if so, how will we handle that?'"

Ralph maintained discipline by ensuring that each time one of his team approached him for advice on a decision, he asked them his simple questions. Soon, each team member had memorized these questions and learned to think and make decisions in that manner. As Ralph explained, "I knew they got it when they would just come into my office, sit down, rattle through the answers to the questions without me saying anything and then make a recommendation."

Ralph also explained to his staff that if they made a decision using this method, he would stand by them even if they made a mistake, because they made a bad decision using a sound method. But if they did not use the method, then he penalized them severely for a bad decision made badly.

In this grey Wolf manner, Ralph combined extreme clarity and extreme discipline to create a delegation framework for the team that made him feel confident that the team always had clear compass points to take them in the right direction. The method gave pack members confidence that they would either succeed or be protected if by chance they failed. By using this tactic, a Wolf CIO can scale up her power by ensuring that the pack understands what the strategic direction is, and how to execute. It enables CIOs to leverage the team to execute consistently and scale the effect to achieve the strategy with minimal waste of effort or resources, and at maximum speed.

Wolves scale up manipulation through coordination and assignation

In the hands of a skilled Machiavellian, even manipulation can be scaled to enterprise proportions. This level of warfare is exceptionally high risk, even for a

Wolf. The more team members the CIO involves in his manipulation strategies, the more likely it is that they will be caught and the strategy will fall apart. So it is essential that the pack be mature and well-formed before the next strategy is attempted. A good test of the health of the pack is to engage them in scaling power in the delegation framework tactic described above. If team members demonstrate that they can work in lockstep consistently, then they are more likely to be candidates for scaling up manipulation through the tactic of mass assignation.

Silvia, a CIO for a logistics agency, described the tactic in the following manner. "Behind closed doors I assemble the team and we plan how to best maneuver the multitude of stakeholders we have to influence to get large-scale change done. We create a highly detailed power map that includes their priorities, relationships, likes, dislikes — even their hobbies and favorite foods. This power map file is encrypted and kept only on my personal laptop, which no one may access but me."

Then she explains, "We continuously analyze their communication styles and who they relate to both on and off the team to determine the best person, channel and information to sway them. If they need to meet with Paul on a project, but they dislike Paul but like Mary, for example, we have Mary set up the meeting and Paul just shows up with her. If they like golf, the information we provide them includes golf analogies.

If they like seafood, I take them out for lunch at the local oyster bar. I learned to do this when I worked for a consumer products company. This is how we analyzed the relationships between multiple target customers at the same time to determine how to sell more, and it made sense to apply it internally here."

As noted, mass assignation is highly risky due to the level of trust and security required among the team. The team must maintain secrecy and discipline and feel confident that they are still behaving ethically in order for the stratagem to succeed. When the wolf pack succeeds, however, the enterprise will view IT not only as strong and able to execute, but also as having exceptional business acumen, people skills and empathy for their peers.

Wolf Packet

The wolf pack is a powerful tool when used well. That power is amplified when they also engage in manipulation on a mass scale. Developing a disciplined pack that can maintain ranks and secrecy under warfare conditions is not easy. But when their Wolf CIO demonstrates clarity, discipline and a mission worth following, strong wolf packs are both possible and a privilege to lead.

Remember:

- Use the IT leadership team to scale up, or rescale them out

- Dolphins must avoid creating teams that are too large to control

- Sharks must avoid accidentally scaling up fear and paralyzing followers

- Wolves demand pack behavior from the pack members

- Wolves scale up power through clarity and discipline

- Wolves scale up manipulation through coordination and assignation

17: Create Strong Alliances to Scale Up, but Select the Appropriate Methods

Whoever has studied ancient history will have found that the republics had three methods of aggrandizement.

One of these was to form a confederation of several republics, neither of which had any eminence over the other in rank or authority;

The second method was to make associates of other states; reserving to themselves, however, the rights of sovereignty, the seat of empire, and the glory of their enterprises.

The third method was to make the conquered people immediately subjects, and not associates.

Of these three methods the latter is perfectly useless.

Machiavelli, *The Discourses*

There are three ways to create alliances: The lower the cost, the greater the risk

Partnership with the rest of the business is the ultimate goal of virtually every CIO. CIOs instinctively understand that creating many relationships between the IT department and other departments is critical to success. We have discussed many elements of that journey here, but the most important component is the complex issue of how exactly to form the partnership to create a powerful alliance or coalition. Machiavelli, upon studying the history of ancient societies, discerned three methods that yield vastly different results. By learning each of these methods and knowing when to apply them, CIOs can succeed in scaling up their sphere of influence and winning the partnership war. There is an inverse relationship between the effort a CIO puts into creating and sustaining the alliance, and the durability of that alliance.

The three methods Machiavelli described are: First, form a partnership of equals in which everyone is treated in the same manner, has an equal say in how the partnership is governed and often make decisions by consensus. Second, create a federation, where there is a strong central authority that governs multiple states, which have some authority of their own. Decisions are made in a blended fashion — the central authority makes some, the states make others and together they make the rest. The third method is to execute a mandate and take over an entire enterprise by force. The states and their people are subjects and the central authority makes all of the decisions. The first method is the domain of the Dolphin, the third the domain of the Shark and the federation is the domain of the Wolf.

Dolphins create alliances of equals that disintegrate on the dark side

Alliances of equals take an enormous amount of time to maintain, but can be worth it in a light-side enterprise where collaboration and transparency are greatly appreciated by the community. Unfortunately, in dark-side enterprises, these alliances tend to be fragile and quickly disintegrate. Consider Serena, a Dolphin CIO of a state in the United States. The governor asked her to find ways to work collaboratively with the counties to save money and find new ways to serve the citizens. Serena wanted all of the county CIOs to feel positively about the shared initiatives and explained her approach as follows. "I convened the CIOs into a governance group and worked hard to get them engaged. We agreed to negotiate all of the initiatives, their priority order, the funding models and the manner in which everyone would participate."

In Serena's situation, every detail of the collaboration approach became subject to negotiation. The county CIOs always found issues in the details and as equals in the fragile alliance, felt empowered to argue each point. After many months of negotiation and re-negotiation, Serena suspected that her colleagues were using the governance forum simply as a stalling tactic to delay having to make real changes. No matter how much additional information she gave them or what she offered them, there was no end in sight to the negotiations, and reaching consensus became impossible. Serena had accidentally created a forum for warfare and large-scale manipulation best referred to as *endless consensus.* Unfortunately, rather than being in control of the manipulation campaign in a Machiavellian fashion, she became both the target and the enabler. Her manipulative colleagues used the forum she created with light-side intentions against her in a dark-side manner.

Sharks favor the all-or-nothing power play, which results in all or nothing

Howard was a university CIO with a Shark approach to warfare. When Howard was hired, the chancellor told him to be innovative and make the university IT more efficient. Howard decided that the best approach to get the quickest results was to seek a mandate to have the entire IT budget centralized and under his control, which had never happened before in the history of the light-side university. Before his start date, Howard asked the president of the university to shift the budget and control to him upon his arrival, and the president agreed. The mandate was a *neutralization strategy*, the Machiavellian equivalent of expansion method three — taking states by force and making them subjects.

When the president broached the topic with the powerful deans of the departments, they balked, and the president quickly reneged on the plan. Unfortunately, when Shark CIOs lose this battle, they also lose the war in just one exchange. The strategy ends up neutralizing them, as they are left appearing weak and vulnerable, experiencing a total power and status drain from which they rarely recover. Colleagues tend to think, *We defeated him when he tried to neutralize us, and so defeating him when he is using smaller weaponry will be even easier. He is clearly not a player so I can ignore him from now on.* Howard left the university soon after he lost the battle and the war.

CIOs who try to force others to participate in a coalition using this method rely on manipulating a single player into lending a massive amount of power to the situation, and have little power of their own from which to draw upon or fall back on. This is an all-or-nothing gamble of the worst kind, because the CIO has virtually no control and is at the mercy of the true power broker. When the neutralize strategy works, the CIO's power increases exponentially. However, those who have been conquered in such a manner become resentful and will always remember the happier days of independence. Therefore, they will never be enthusiastic or loyal to the Shark CIO, and can be expected to continuously engage in mass resistance as long as he is in power.

When the tactic fails, the Shark's power is drained entirely, and even extreme manipulation won't save him. So CIOs must use great caution when exercising neutralization to scale up their territory. It works best in dark, Shark-filled cultures where the players not only expect massive power plays, but tend to only respect those who can actually pull them off. In any other type of culture, CIOs should test the CEO's and CFO's willingness to lend them their power by requesting smaller power plays first, to see if they can or will follow through, before betting the entire IT shop on this risky all-or-nothing stratagem.

Wolves use multilateral strategies in federated environments

Few CIOs live in either light-side collaborative cultures or extreme dark-side aggressive cultures. Most CIOs live in federated environments where they are better served by applying multiple grey Wolf CIOs strategies that combine power and manipulation to create durable alliances. Wolf CIOs are selective about who they consider for an alliance and recognize that not every business unit is an equally good candidate. They understand also that each member of the alliance should not have the same role or influence. As discussed earlier, partnership involves parties of approximately the same power and status who invest similarly in the relationship and share both the risks and the rewards. This is particularly important to note when a CIO scales up and engages multiple partners at the same time in an alliance. Wolf CIOs treat those with different power and status levels differently.

Consider Lauren, the Wolf CIO of a federated, multinational semiconductor company, engaged in an ERP initiative. The enterprise had a mix of large and small business units, with radically different contributions to revenue and margin, and multiple ERP systems that needed consolidation. ERP requires strong, long-term, highly engaged coalitions in order to be successful. Large numbers of stakeholders must work together to decide when to redesign business processes and when to customize the technology, otherwise the initiative will fail. Lauren began the campaign by garnering support for the consolidated ERP approach using what can best be referred to as the *mathematical steamroller* approach.

As she explained, "Getting people to agree to give up control is like math; order matters. I create an initial talk track or business case and then I select a colleague to practice it on. Usually, it is someone who has a small ERP project that would be subsumed in the consolidation and I try to get their support for the change. If I succeed in convincing them, then my test has been successful. If I fail to get their support, then I haven't lost significant ground as they are not a major player or influencer. I use them to fine tune my talk track, and continue to do so until I can get the minor player on board."

Once she secures the minor player, then the more complex steamroller math begins. "I move on to the welterweight colleagues who are more likely to be resistant, and try to get some of them on board. Then I have to figure out which of the heavyweights to go after next. Some of them are high status and will only support the initiative if they are the first high-status person on board because they want to be seen as leading the charge. If there are too many welterweights already in the alliance, the first heavyweight will shy away as it will seem like a low-status initiative, but a few are ok. Then finally there are the heavyweights who will only come on board when a critical mass of their other heavyweight peers are already signed on. As long as I can manage the math, I can create a strong support system for the ERP initiative." By applying the mathematical steamroller, CIOs can scale up their manipulations and incrementally power up the alliance to maximum strength and efficacy. Get the math wrong, and the entire alliance dissipates.

Wolves maximize the minority to maintain a durable alliance

A common error many CIOs make in an alliance is using extreme, all-or-nothing approaches once they are formed, and inadvertently compromising the partnership. Consider again the example of an ERP project.

Once Lauren had formed a strong alliance, it would be tempting to use that success to force a single instance of the ERP or to create a single funding model to simplify the approach. Unfortunately, large alliances can rarely succeed with such rigid approaches, so they must be adaptable and open to solutions that maximize the minority — essential to federated enterprise success. Wolf CIOs try to limit the complexity of federated models without going to extremes.

Once the alliance is formed, treating the minority as though they are lower in status and power will poison the partnership environment. For example, if the smaller players would be disproportionately damaged by the chargeback system, financial adjustments should be made rather than allowing the majority to design a one-size-fits-all approach that benefits them. If one version of the ERP system is untenable for everyone, then having two versions is a better approach than allowing the alliance to disintegrate back to many more versions. Wolf CIOs know that success in a federated model involves engaging in just enough complexity to take care of the majority and minority, but no more and no less.

Wolves are opportunistic and make the most of each crisis

Wolves recognize when an opportunity presents itself to form alliances quickly and get people to work together who normally would not. Earlier we discussed the high-risk neutralization strategy of the Shark, which scales up quickly through the use of massive force, but often ends in disaster. The Wolf CIO uses the *optimization strategy*, which starts with a disaster or potential disaster, but ends with an alliance. It turns dark days for the enterprise into a collaborative light-side outcome quickly.

The optimization strategy takes advantage of one of two critical situations where the enterprise is in such crisis that business units are willing to give over control rapidly and work together to protect their very survival. The first is after a new competitor enters the market and changes the business model so radically that the enterprise cannot continue to operate as it had in the past and survive. Technologies have also driven this kind of change; for example, digital media, which has profoundly impacted multiple industries. The second is after a natural disaster creates havoc in the enterprise.

One CIO shared the impact of a hurricane on his enterprise. "Prior to the storm, we operated in a very decentralized manner. We had lots of customers and efficiency was not an issue. After the region was devastated by a storm, we had to become very lean very quickly to survive and attract customers back. After the region recovered and business grew, we continued to operate in the same manner because we had done it together and saw how well it worked." This Wolf CIO displayed the adaptability needed to optimize in a disastrous situation and use the spontaneous team-work to make the changes durable and high value for the enterprise.

Wolf Packet

Strong partnerships and alliances are critical to CIOs scaling up and they should not extend that relationship to others lightly. Consider vendors, who CIOs often refer to as partners. While a light-side CIO can partner with many light-side vendors, they must always factor in two variables. Once again, getting the math right matters. First, when some vendor representatives are under heavy quota pressure, they can quickly go to the dark side. Second, vendors are rarely of the same power and status as your enterprise. If the vendor generates exponentially more revenue than you do and is on the dark side, you are not partners. In this case you may be a customer, perhaps a hostage, and in the extreme, some CIOs become vendor cult members, but you are not partners. Always examine the mathematical reality of the power dynamics and do not use, or allow others to use, the partner terminology lightly.

Remember:

- There are three ways to create alliances; the lower the cost, the greater the risk
- Dolphins create alliances of equals that disintegrate on the dark side
- Sharks favor the all-or-nothing power play, which results in all or nothing
- Wolves use multilateral strategies in federated environments
- Wolves maximize the minority to maintain a durable alliance
- Wolves are opportunistic and make the most of each crisis

18: Fight on Multiple Fronts to Avoid Being Boxed in by the Enemy or Yourself

A general who disposes his army in such manner that it can rally three times in the course of a battle, must have fortune against him three times before being defeated, and must have an enemy opposed to him sufficiently superior to overcome him three times.

But if an army can resist only a single shock, it may easily lose the battle; for with the slightest disorder even the most mediocre courage may carry off the victory.

Machiavelli, *The Discourses*

Scale up your capacity by always fighting on multiple fronts, but not too many

Succeeding in warfare requires knowing when to go beyond fighting the wars on the fronts that we have been asked to fight, and fighting the wars that need to be fought. As Machiavelli explained, generals who fight battles with a single battle line will collapse as soon as the line is broken by the enemy. But those who think multilaterally and have at least three battle lines are strong enough to recover, regroup, move forward and win the war. All CIOs must fight on at least three fronts — top-line growth, bottom-line savings and risk mitigation — which represent the most coveted victories for most enterprises. A CIO who fights on only one of these fronts risks having nothing left to fall back on should she fail. And should she succeed on the one front alone, the victory may be too narrow to protect the CIO or the enterprise should the other two fail due to a competitor's attack or just bad luck.

Consider that a CIO who succeeds in creating cost savings alone may be seen as reliable but not strategic. A CIO who only delivers growth may be seen as strategic but not reliable. And those who deliver risk mitigation may be seen as reliable, but not innovative. At the same time, CIOs must be cautious not to fight on too many fronts at the same time. By taking on too many battles and overreaching, a CIO at the front lines will be weak in all areas. Wolf CIOs are strong on at least one front, and marshal their forces to be good enough at the other two to protect themselves, the IT team and the enterprise.

Dolphins let themselves get boxed in and limit their opportunities for growth

Ari is a Dolphin CIO in a Southeast Asian government agency that processes benefits checks for unemployed citizens. Ari was asked to consolidate the disparate infrastructure and applications, and was told by his department head that this was his "only" priority. Although Ari had an extensive background in innovative and customer-facing systems, he honored his department head's request to focus all of his time and energy on the top enterprise objective of consolidation and cost savings. After two years of hard work and intensive collaboration with his colleagues, Ari completed the consolidation as requested and achieved the stated cost-savings targets.

Soon thereafter he was let go by his department head. When a stunned Ari asked the executive why, she explained that while she appreciated the work that Ari had done, the next phase of change in the enterprise would be dedicated to transformation and innovation, and she did not believe that Ari was the right person to lead this. By following the direction of his department head and fighting on the cost-savings front exclusively, Ari became complicit in branding himself as "the cost-savings CIO" rather than as "the innovative CIO." Ari's error was fighting the war only on the cost-savings front, and not reserving some of his forces for more innovative battlefronts to protect himself, the team and the enterprise from all sides.

Sharks are suspicious and fight on the fronts their colleagues prefer they avoid

Natalie is a Shark CIO who joined a federated manufacturing company that had never had a global CIO.

She realized that there were many opportunities for different geographical business units to work together, but for cultural reasons they were working independently. She consulted with the business-unit presidents to get their input into where she might focus her efforts. Each of them advised her to focus on commodity applications and consolidating the procurement process. While there was some business benefit to taking on these large initiatives, Natalie was concerned that they were steering her away from the strategic IT they wanted to protect and keep to themselves, and thus were trying to distract her and keep her busy.

Natalie refused to be distracted and decided to leverage her reporting relationship with the CFO, who was anxious to get control over IT spending and find new sources of revenue. He agreed that she should review and sign off on any IT-related purchases in each of the regions before the funds would be allocated to find opportunities to optimize the investments. In retaliation, the business-unit heads quietly banded together in an act of mass manipulation and submitted their IT requests one week before the budget deadline. They ensured that the CIO would not have time to review them, and believed that the CFO would sign off on everything rather than slowing the budgeting process down. They were mistaken. The CFO rejected all the requests and set aside funding for Natalie to allocate only after the requests were reviewed.

Natalie successfully fended off two mass manipulations that would have boxed her in by pulling off a large-scale power play with the CFO. In doing so, she successfully devised a way to influence every IT front in the enterprise. But the aggressive Shark tactic created an oversight relationship between the global CIO and business units, which Shark CIO Natalie must take care to moderate with light-side tactics. Otherwise, in the extreme, repeating the massive power play will inhibit trust even further, and trigger increased conflict between the CIO and the mass manipulators in the business units.

Wolf CIOs choose to fight the wars no one thought to fight

The most effective war fighters are innovators at heart who take the actions that no one expected to deliver previously unimagined value. Penny, the CIO of a property management group specializing in theaters and arenas, is such a Wolf. Her CEO and CFO viewed IT as a cost center, and encouraged her to focus on creating cost savings and clean audit reports, which the Dolphin side of Penny agreed to do. But Penny decided to break the mold and go to the Shark side as well to also take on the growth and innovation fronts.

Penny explains her approach: "I took my IT leadership team to several venues to actually work the events and service paying customers with the sales, marketing and events teams. Many of them had never done this before, only going to the venues off hours to implement IT. They started to understand challenges with the IT systems that they could not understand previously, and would have been difficult for others to articulate to them. They were then able to identify innovative opportunities for technology to improve the customer experience and sales through better information management and business intelligence."

Enterprises that view IT as a cost center sometimes try to keep the CIO and IT in the back office to fight the back-office wars. Few IT departments are invited to work with the paying customers directly, and even fewer invite themselves. This is a huge opportunity lost for IT and for the enterprise. Fortunately, there is a solution for this. CIOs must get out of the back office and go fight at the front office whenever possible. Colleagues, although they may be initially skeptical, will grow to appreciate IT proactively investing time in customers, innovation and revenue growth. By crossing the territorial boundary, CIOs and their teams can scale up their impact by better understanding which technology weapon to hand their colleagues to grow more revenue. And by doing so, they can win the war to evolve from order taker to true partner.

Grey Wolves move into the front with the grey space and take over

Adventurous Wolves expand their battlefronts and territories well outside of IT by taking advantage of opportunities that others tend to ignore. What do you do as a CIO when you encounter a grey space that no one in your enterprise seems to be in charge of? Most enterprises have many in-between spaces that no one manages either because of turnover, or because the specialty area is emerging and the enterprise is unaware of the opportunity or has yet to deal with it. Areas such as innovation, business process improvement and information management often fit into the grey spaces. When I asked one group of CIOs what they do when they encounter a grey space, one entertaining CIO emphatically responded: "We put a server in it!"

Consider Leonard, a Wolf CIO for a professional services company where no one was in charge of business process improvement. Unlike many companies that have a COO for this purpose, Leonard's company had none. As he and his team proceeded with several large-scale IT initiatives, the lack of leadership in this area became an execution challenge. Leonard decided to move into the grey space. He explained, "I decided to take over business process improvement. I didn't ask permission, and I didn't tell anyone, I just did it and it became so. Many of my team had experience in this area from being in IT for so many years. So I began assigning my team members to key business capabilities, and had them map the business processes, working with their colleagues in the business unit. Then, they led both the scoping work for the new IT related to each process, and helped set performance improvement targets for their new areas. After some time and a number of highly visible successes, I incorporated the new roles into their and my job descriptions and we officially owned the space."

Wolf CIOs recognize the military reality that the easiest hill to take is the one not occupied by the enemy. As long as it is a high-value hill, it is worth pursuing. Wolves spend little time worrying about who *should* be in charge of something, or how things are *supposed to be* or what *tradition* says about roles. They look for the grey spaces and move the front there to scale up their reach and range, and secure more value for the enterprise.

Wolf Packet

The critical battlefronts for CIOs are top-line growth, bottom-line savings and risk mitigation. CIOs must be able to master at least one, and scale their forces to take on the other two well enough. Most importantly, Wolf CIOs must be willing to scale outside of the traditional box and outside of IT and into the grey spaces, where opportunity often lies.

Remember:

- Scale up your capacity by always fighting on multiple fronts, but not too many
- Dolphins let themselves get boxed in and limit their opportunities for growth
- Sharks are suspicious and fight on the fronts their colleagues prefer they avoid
- Wolf CIOs break tradition and choose the wars no one thought to fight
- Grey Wolves move into the front with the grey space and take over

19: Create Weapons of Mass Destruction Through Force Multiplication

There is nothing as likely to succeed as what the enemy believes you cannot attempt.

Machiavelli, *The Art of War*

Sometimes the alternative is that there is no alternative

The ultimate weapons are weapons of mass destruction (WMDs). CIOs must sometimes combine massive manipulation with massive power to achieve a force multiplier effect and create a cataclysmic weapon. The use of such weapons in the world of warfare requires a Wolf CIO with a healthy appetite for risk and an exceptional degree of control. The tactics described here scale up even further than our previous extreme tactics, by going outside the enterprise, to the board or the public, or outside of traditional leadership mindsets to amplify the CIO's Machiavellian abilities even farther. As Machiavelli noted, the best strategy is often the one that no one believes you will undertake because it is either so high risk or so destructive that it is hard to imagine anyone actually implementing it. But sometimes, there is no alternative.

Whether CIOs deploy a WMD as the final step in an escalation pattern of tactics, or as a first salvo against a much stronger enemy, they must be careful not to accidentally incinerate whatever they were fighting for in the first place. Dolphin CIOs would almost never deploy such a weapon, and Sharks might enjoy them a bit too much. Therefore, only Wolves should place their finger on the big red button, as only they are adept at using these immensely dark tactics to shine some light.

An auditor is a force multiplier with a spreadsheet

Daniel, a CIO at an international grocery company, was faced with the possibility of accidentally deploying a WMD. He agreed to take the CIO job fully aware that the scope of his role included having control over only half of the IT budget and staff. The other half of the IT staff was not accountable to him and was dispersed throughout the rest of the business. Two weeks after his arrival, the auditors, preparing a report for the board of directors (who Daniel had not yet met), asked him if he thought IT was cost-effective and compliant with all the appropriate regulations.

Daniel did not believe that IT was either cost-effective or compliant, but was reluctant to say so. As a new hire at the organization, he had no idea how the board or CEO would react to his telling the truth in the situation. In his experience, while CEOs prefer that auditors have "the truth," there was always the matter of when and how much truth to give them. He decided to tell the auditor the truth as he knew it from his limited experience with the company, *No, he did not believe it was possible that the enterprise was compliant. No, he had no visibility into the decentralized IT investment. Yes, he was concerned that the business units lacked the proper IT skills to assure compliance. No, there did not seem to be any standards as his colleagues seemed to buy what they wanted. No, he could not say that appropriate controls were in place. No, he did not think that they were cost-effective or positioned for growth. Was he concerned about their competitive position? Yes, though he was probably too new to know for certain yet.* He braced himself for the fallout.

The next week the auditor attended the board meeting. Daniel did not. The day after the conclusion of the meeting, the CEO called Daniel into his office. Expecting the worst, Daniel was surprised to hear the CEO say, "Daniel, the entire IT staff now reports to you, and you have accountability for the entire IT budget. I'm not comfortable with the risks you and the auditor pointed out, and we are taking immediate action to deal with the situation." Daniel was an accidental Wolf CIO. He had inadvertently deployed a WMD and staged a bloodless coup by engaging the auditor and telling him what others had feared to say. In this case, the auditor's spreadsheet was a WMD when shared with the board of directors, and the CIO's best friend in a war of expansion.

Some CIOs deliberately go to the board to report what they consider significant IT-related challenges or risks that they have been unable to address through the enterprise leadership or other channels. Success is not always assured and can be a career-ending or limiting move if the board does not agree or appreciate their shedding light on a situation. Had the board or CEO reacted differently, the outcome might have been much worse for Daniel. Thanks to its success, he helped protect the enterprise and avoid the ravages of a long-term battle to gain control of the situation and assure regulatory compliance.

The press and the threat of public scrutiny are exponential force multipliers

As powerful as an auditor and board can be, tapping into the public opinion of millions is exponentially more effective. Michaela is the Wolf CIO of a large governmental region. A political leader announced a massive IT-related integration project that would be completed in 12 months. He specifically designated Michaela's office as being in charge of the ambitious initiative. The first time that Michaela heard about the project was at the press conference. She immediately approached the political leader and told him she was willing to do everything she could to meet his objective. However, she was short-staffed and over capacity just covering the current portfolio of IT initiatives, so she needed money and consultants to complete the ambitious project. The political leader refused, with the imperious directive, "Just make it happen!"

Some light-side CIOs would have moved heaven and earth to find a way to make the project happen with no additional resources. They would believe that the politician's public announcement served to trap them and place their reputations on the line. While this may be true, Michaela was Wolf enough to use the press conference to place the noose around the politician's neck. She realized that the politician's reputation was more publicly on the line than her own. So she decided to use a Wolf tactic, best described as tightening the noose, around the politician. Each time the politician asked her for an update, she told him that they were in fact trying their best, but with no additional resource, the project would likely not hit the announced target.

Predictably, the politician periodically reminded her to make it happen, and she continued to tell him that they were doing their best, but would not likely hit the target. Then, she informed the politician that the press had requested an interview with her to discuss the exciting initiative. The politician began to panic, and Michaela turned up the pressure by telling him what she planned to say to the press and millions of constituents. *What would she tell the press? Why the truth, of course, since the politician would not ask her to lie, would he? No, she could not avoid talking with the press. She had said yes to the interview and her can-celling it would not be right. Yes, she would have to tell them that the project was started with no funding and no staff if they asked her. But miracles in IT do sometimes happen, don't they?*

As the press bore down, and the news became increasingly skeptical of the looming deadline, the politician "suddenly" came up with the idea to pro-vide substantial consulting resources and funding to the project. While light-side CIOs would be loath to use the press and public exposure in such a manner, Michaela recognized how powerful they could be in this situation. Like a well-balanced grey Wolf, she did not inappropriately initiate contact with the press or leak any information to them. She simply recog-nized that the politician had handed her a WMD and she used it against him rather than allowing the target to be placed on her. The project was executed on time, and the politician became a hero who the grateful populace reelected. And Michaela, the Wolf CIO, stayed on through his next term to help the politician continue to make things happen. Fortu-nately, few CIOs need to go this far to get the desired result. Often just the implied threat of *What would the public think?* is enough to gain the desired effect.

Sometimes the most powerful weapon is the patience to let foes self-destruct

One of the most difficult challenges for a Wolf CIO is to know when to take the extreme measure of sending the troops back to the barracks, and let the enemy self-destruct. Then the only thing left to do is pick up the pieces afterward. Sometimes, when a dark-side culture requires extreme intervention, it is an indication that it is too damaged to salvage and a CIO's actions will only forestall the inevitable. This will draw out the battle and the war, resulting in more casualties on both sides while changing little else. A strong leader will be reluctant to allow this to happen, but will recognize that scaling all the way back and allowing the conflict to take its course may be the most merciful choice.

Consider this situation as described by a Wolf CIO: "I became the CIO of a dysfunctional not-for-profit charity where all the staff had been there for a long time. They refused to do virtually any work, and had no sense of urgency. I had worked at other charities where staff worked hard to execute the mission, and were innovators and positive contributors, but in this organization, there was no glimmer of that kind of behavior. I tried everything to help them progress, but when nothing worked, I decided to let them fail. I stopped protecting them and making excuses for them, and allowed multiple IT failures, security breaches and other issues to come to light. Then I recommended that the entire department be outsourced and the leadership agreed. It was not the outcome that I wanted, but I realized I had only been delaying the inevitable to the detriment of the important mission of the organization."

Such situations are not unique to a single industry and appear in many enterprises where dark forces have so thoroughly corrupted the environment that they overpower any Wolf CIO's ability to win a war through either power or manipulation. These extreme dark situations are not unique to the IT department, and often apply to cross-business-unit initiatives and teams that are so flawed they are impervious to almost any tactics, light or dark. Then the best course of action for the enterprise is to allow them to fall under their own dark weight, and set a new course of action. In these extreme cases, a Wolf CIO will recognize that the best way to win the war is to allow the enemy to lose it.

Wolf Packet

CIOs who learn to scale up their power and manipulation tactics can succeed at warfare. Successful Wolf CIOs build their strengths and skills, plan their campaigns carefully, and take advantage of the good luck that may resemble your enemy inadvertently handing you a weapon to use against them. Effective warfare requires the ability to inspire followership and the selflessness to do the most difficult things — all in the hope of bringing the enterprise out of a dark war and into a light-filled peace.

Remember:

- Sometimes the alternative is that there is no alternative
- An auditor is a force multiplier with a spreadsheet
- The press and the threat of public scrutiny are exponential force multipliers
- Sometimes the most powerful weapon is the patience to let enemies self-destruct
- In extreme cases, a Wolf CIO will recognize that the best way to win the war is to allow the enemy to lose it

We have explored the dark side of leadership in the three Machiavellian disciplines of power, manipulation and warfare, and the good that can come from using these tactics. Do you still want to be a Wolf? At the beginning of this journey you became an honorary member of the Machiavellian Wolf Pack by deciding to read this book. Now, if you still want to be a Wolf CIO, and more importantly the head of your own wolf pack, you must apply the wisdom of those who have come before you, and do some things differently today — and each today after that.

Let's take the next steps together.

Light Dark

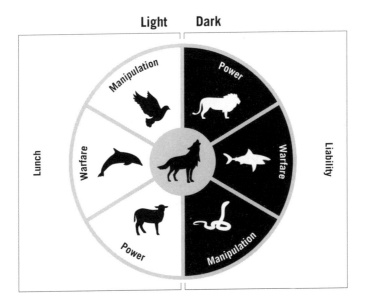

Today

Men are ever more taken with the things of the present than with those of the past;

And when they find their own good in the present, then they enjoy it and seek none other, and will be ready in every way to defend the new prince, provided he be not wanting to himself in other respects.

And thus he will have the double glory of having established a new principality, and of having strengthened and adorned it with good laws, good armies, good allies, and good examples.

Machiavelli, *The Prince*

20: Put One Paw in Front of the Other

Whoever, then, in a newly acquired state, finds it necessary, to secure himself against his enemies, to gain friends, to conquer by force or by cunning, to make himself feared or beloved by the people,

to be followed and revered by the soldiery, to destroy all who could or might injure him, to substitute a new for the old order of things,

to be severe and yet gracious, magnanimous, and liberal, to disband a disloyal army and create a new one,

to preserve the friendship of kings and princes, so that they may bestow benefits upon him with grace, and fear to injure him.

Machiavelli, *The Prince*

This is your final Wolf Packet

Throughout this exploration of Machiavelli and the Extreme Animal Ecosystem, we have challenged you to go to the dark side and consider tactics that are rarely discussed in polite company. Leadership and warfare are rarely polite, and often they are rather ugly. But when a CIO succeeds in dealing with dark-side issues, it is often for the benefit of many. This final Wolf Packet includes reminders of the key principles, suggests actions for you to take today, and presents guidelines to consider as you continue the journey to becoming a stronger Wolf Pack leader.

Appreciate the animal that you are today

While reading this book you have likely discovered that you have a number of Wolf-like traits, but perhaps more closely resemble another animal. Discovering your dominant style is an important part of the journey. Start by taking the assessment that accompanies this book at www.gartner.com/wolfcio and determine your Extreme Animal Profile. Recognize the strengths of that profile and strive to build your toolkit so that you can be a Wolf CIO when you need to be.

If you are in a light-side enterprise and culture, you are fortunate

Avoid using dark-side tactics aggressively in light-side cultures. They can corrupt positive, collaborative behaviors and make the CIO stand out in a negative light. However, even in light-side cultures, the CIO must monitor individual stakeholders who may practice dark-side behaviors and take appropriate countermeasures. Although traditional management philosophy suggests that looking for dark behaviors may be a self-fulfilling prophesy, Machiavelli would suggest that those who do not look for them are sure to be caught unprepared and unable to defend themselves.

Spend too much time on the light side and risk becoming lunch

Although CIOs should always strive to be on the light side, they must recognize that when the enterprise or powerful individuals in it tend to the dark side, light-side strategies are dangerous. Light-side CIOs may be perceived as good, but they may also be perceived as weak or prey, and at risk of becoming a predator's lunch.

Spend too much time on the dark side and risk becoming a liability

Dark-side behaviors are essential to CIO success, especially when dealing with a dark-side environment. But when CIOs spend too much time on the dark side they risk being perceived as bad, destructive or self-serving, and may become tagged as a liability who must be eliminated.

The grey Wolf always has one paw on the light side and one paw in the dark

As Machiavelli explained, leadership is filled with contradictions. A CIO's ability to carefully walk the line of light and dark will determine if she will grow into a grey Wolf, or fall into a bright or dark abyss. A great Wolf CIO always uses light-side tactics when they are effective, but will use the dark side when they need to and can ensure a light-side outcome.

Aspiring Wolves must go to the extremes to strengthen the middle

Unfortunately, the path to stronger CIO leadership is not a straight line that begins with relative weakness and ends with moderation. When weaker leaders use power or manipulation in moderation, they are perceived as weak leaders who are trying to be strong. A Wolf CIO visibly uses extreme dark-side tactics such as those of the Lion, Snake and Shark. Then, when he applies more moderate grey Wolf tactics, he appears to be a formidable predator who is reining in his tremendous strength and being magnanimous or merciful. Thus the path to becoming a strong Wolf leadership is one of radiating out to the extremes, then returning to the grey space.

A Wolf is neither a power Lamb nor Lion, but both at the same time

Power is ethically neutral. CIOs can wield it for good or for bad, but if they do not have it they cannot use it to protect themselves or others for whom they are responsible. Lambs strive to be liked, and but have few other defenses. Lions strive to be seen as getting things done, but may frighten others while doing it. Wolves find the balance of being likeable enough, yet assertive enough, to get the job done. And, when a larger Wolf threatens, they know when to be a Lamb and live to fight another day.

A Wolf is neither a manipulation Dove nor Snake, but both at the same time

Power is not always effective, particularly in the face of a manipulative enemy who makes it difficult for a powerful CIO to know where to strike. When CIOs use light-side techniques to get their way, it is influence. When they use dark-side techniques, it is manipulation. Doves have strong, immutable value systems, but may seem unyielding or impractical to others. Snakes are adaptable and adjust their tactic to the situation, but may appear untrustworthy to others. Wolves find the balance by having a strong value system, but knowing that the values of others may differ. They use manipulation to ensure that they do not become victims of it themselves.

A Wolf is neither a warfare Dolphin nor Shark, but both at the same time

The territory of CIOs is subject to invasion from other business units and external competitors. So CIOs must know how to defend themselves, and wage offensive wars when appropriate, to help grow their businesses. Therefore they must learn how to scale up power and manipulation tactics and conduct campaigns involving multiple fronts at the same time. Dolphins gain followership by caring about the community, but have few tools when the community falls apart. Sharks kill with extreme prejudice and gain followership by winning, but they risk terrorizing their own followers and potential allies. Wolf CIOs care enough to create loyalty among their followers, but are willing to create mass destruction and press the big red button when they have no other alternative.

If you are in a hostile situation today, it may be your fault. So what?

In reading this book, you may have realized that your own behaviors may have contributed to the situation you are in now. This is evidence that you are not alone, and that there was little reason you should have figured this out before now. So what? Continue putting one paw in front of the other in the right direction. If you have been the problem, do not let that get in your way. The good news is that you have control over your own actions, and therefore can course-correct. It is much more difficult to change the behaviors of others than to change our own.

Conflict is often a sign of success, so embrace it

Leaders must embrace the reality that often conflict is a sign of success. Being ignored is much more dangerous. As a leader, you have something they want so you're a target. Alternatively, the players may have changed or may now be under duress. Wolf CIOs focus on staying calm when others are trying to create chaos or knock them off balance. During a conflict, he who loses control of himself loses the battle. Those who rarely engage in battle are most likely to lose control. So embrace conflict and engage; practice does make perfect.

You will make mistakes; the objective is not perfection

As you try different power, manipulation and warfare techniques, it is certain you will make mistakes. If you do not make any mistakes, you may not be taking enough risk. If everything starts exploding around you, you may have accidentally jumped into the deep end of the pool and you need to start treading water. Remember that the difference between taking a risk and being reckless is being thoughtful and analyzing your options based on risk, reward and collateral damage. Do not allow perfectionism to confuse you or cause you to panic. Most mistakes are recoverable and will help you gather information and expand your own tolerance for risk.

The Wolf CIO is not always meant to win

If you fail or have failed in the past, there may be a reason. When Wolf CIOs feel compelled to apply extreme techniques continuously, the environment may be toxic and beyond redemption. In such situations, get out of the enterprise if you can. If you cannot due to financial realities or other constraints, remember that Machiavelli was nothing if not pragmatic. Focus on defensive tactics and hope for a shift in the culture to the light side.

Take inspiration from other parts of your life

Consider which animal you are in your private life or in different roles you play in your community. It is not unusual to find CIOs who are Wolves at home, but light-side animals at work because of the long tradition of light-side IT practices. Many CIOs easily manipulate their children and inspire fear in them when necessary. *Do not touch that light socket! No, you may not eat the entire box of cookies! Yes, Santa Claus is real and is always watching you, so you need to behave.* Consider the powerful and thoughtful stance you use in other parts of your life and consider applying the same skill sets and inspiration to your role as a CIO. These techniques will work because most children never grow up, they just get taller.

If you don't like the rules, they are probably yours, so change them

Many of the rules we live by are self-imposed. And while they serve a strong purpose for a period of time, we must recognize when those rules either become outdated or do not apply to our situation. Rules such as *always be transparent, always be completely honest, never use power against others* and *avoid creating collateral damage,* each have their utility and are grounded in good intentions, but can lead us astray and into defeat. When dealing with a difficult situation, always challenge your rules and assumptions to ensure that you do not inadvertently limit your options for success.

Don't ask permission to be a Wolf CIO; just become one

As you place one paw in front of the other, you will begin to see results. Success can be measured in the difference in how your colleagues will look at you, and in how they treat you and the IT department. It can be measured in terms of the increased business results you will be able to create by delivering greater top line, bottom line and risk mitigation to the enterprise. It can be measured in your increased feeling of control and ability to find options to help succeed in even the most difficult situations. The journey may have been a dark one, but you will see the light at the end of the tunnel and walk through it.

Above all else, be worthy of being followed

One of the most compelling Machiavellian concepts is his reference of the ancient concept of Virtu'. In some translations, this word is defined as virtue. While this does convey some of what the concept intended, the actual definition of Virtu' is *worthy of being followed*. Machiavelli believed that leadership was a privilege and a burden, but not a right. He believed that ethics are not optional and leaders have to be willing to do what is best for their people and the republic, and risk themselves in the process. They have to be willing to fight to create something of worth, and then be willing to fight to protect what they created.

Great leaders will wake up and ask themselves, *Am I worthy of being followed today?* Wolf CIOs and aspiring Wolves can answer yes, but they will always have enough healthy doubt in themselves to ask the question again the next day.

Now, proudly repeat after me...

I would rather be a Wolf. I can be a Wolf. I will practice being a Wolf.

And before you know it, you will be able to say, "I am a Wolf CIO."

Acknowledgements

My thanks to the reviewers who told me the good, the bad and the ugly along the way and continuously held me to their extremely high standards: Leslie Brennan, Beverly Tramontelli, Audrey Apfel, Will Hahn, Bill Caffery, Diane Morello, Ken McGee, Andy Rowsell-Jones and Janice van Reyk.

To Dale Kutnick, for relentlessly encouraging me over the years to get this book done, and for telling me what my voice sounds like.

Many thanks to Heather Pemberton Levy, who coached and cajoled me through the process and challenged me to say what I really wanted to say.

Thank you to the amazing Gartner marketing, editing, design and production team led by Monica Virag for their creative energy and willingness to go to the dark side.

Special thanks to Andrew Spender for his support of this project, lending his resources and his enthusiasm every step of the way.

And most importantly, my thanks to the many CIOs who generously shared their challenges, successes and Machiavellian strategies so that others could benefit from their experiences.

About the Author

Tina Nunno is a research vice president and Gartner Fellow at Gartner, Inc., the world's largest information technology research and advisory company, responsible for conducting research and developing publications aimed at helping CIOs and their organizations globally, to improve their performance and contribution. She specializes in CIO-related management issues including working with the board of directors, executive communication strategies, change leadership and enterprise governance strategies.

Ms. Nunno's most recent research deals with navigating complex CIO decisions and sensitive organizational politics issues. She focuses on specific strategies and tactics for managing IT political land mines, power dynamics and the politics of partnering with the rest of the business. She presents as a keynote speaker at conferences around the world, has co-authored Gartner's Annual CIO survey research and is one of the founders of Gartner's global Women's CIO Community. Ms. Nunno has a degree in history from Yale University, and an M.P.A. from American University in Washington, D.C.

Read Tina's blog at blogs.gartner.com/tina-nunno.